Thomas Ulrich

MADE FOR ONE ANOTHER

SOUL MATES
IN FICTION AND IN REAL LIFE

Bluestar
Communications®

Woodside, California

Translated by Howard Fine

First published in German under the title
Dualseelen
© 1996 Aquamarin Verlag, Grafing

This translation:
© 1998 Bluestar Communications Corporation
44 Bear Glenn
Woodside, CA 94062
Tel: 800-6-Bluestar

Edited by Jude Berman
Cover Art by Sulamith Wülfing,
Layout: Petra Michel

Copyright Cover Illustration:
© 1998 S. Wülfing B.V. Amsterdam
First printing 1998
ISBN: 1-885394-26-8

Library of Congress Cataloging-in-Publication Data
Ulrich, Thomas, 1962-
    [Dualseelen. English]
    Made for one another : soulmates in fiction and in real life / Thomas
Ulrich : [translated by Howard Fine].
        p.   cm.
    Includes bibliographical references (p.   ).
    ISBN 1-885394-26-8
    1. Soul mates in literature.   2. Religion and literature.
3. Interpersonal relations.   4. Soul mates.   I. Title.
    PN56.S666U5713   1998
    291.2'2--dc21   97-37736
                                                                  CIP

Printed in USA

CONTENTS

Gently, with the twist of this delicate band,
We're joined, you and I, forever, 'tis true.
I've been sent from some faraway, strange land,
Only to be healed through union with you.

The band between us is snarled and askew;
No one can unravel it, no one but you.
Not 'til you finally succeed,
Can we both be healed and freed.

Ephides

Excerpted with the cordial consent of Anthos Publishers Weinheim, Germany from *Ephides—Ein Dichter des Transzendenten* (*Ephides— A Transcendental Poet*).

8

INTRODUCTION

Most likely, you have at least heard about the concept of "soul mates." Of course, different people are liable to have different ideas about what the words "soul mates" really mean.

Soul mates (also known as "twin souls," "dual souls" and "soul companions") are two souls—one embodying the male principle, the other embodying the female principle—that have belonged together since time immemorial. Two souls of this sort are described as a "pair of souls" or as "two halves of the same person." The doctrine of soul mates claims that for every man there exists a corresponding woman (his original, sole and genuine mate) and, vice versa, for every woman there exists a corresponding man.

Unfortunately, the ancient knowledge about soul mates has been almost entirely forgotten in our present era. Although so-called modern people seldom occupy themselves with mystical questions—and, thus, no longer understand the primordial unity of soul mates—this does not mean that this primal wisdom has been entirely lost. It has survived in the human subconscious, as we can see by examining the many figures of speech, the original meanings of which may no longer be known to us, but that nonetheless confirm this wisdom. For example, we sometimes talk about two people who were "made for one another" or who were "fated for one another." The figure of speech "there's a pot for every cover" likewise expresses this view. A husband often refers to his wife as "my better half." In Kenneth Branagh's gripping reincarnation thriller "Dead Again," a newly wedded husband places a bracelet around his wife's ankle and explains its symbolism to her: "When a man puts this chain around his wife's ankle, it means that from now on they are no longer two separate beings, but have become one. They are two halves of the same person, two halves of a single whole, and not even death can separate them." These few words express more or less everything there is to say about soul mates.

Soul mates are truly two halves of a primordial whole. The doctrine of soul mates assumes that a corresponding counterpart originally existed for every woman and every man. According to this doctrine, paired souls belonged together and represented, in their united condition, "the human being in a state of wholeness and completion." The Bible (Genesis 1:27) expresses this as follows: "So God created man in His own image; in the image of God, created He him; male and female, created He them." According to the Sohar, this "human being in a state of wholeness and completion" is the only being who "truly deserves to be called human." The primordial human dyad unifies the male and female principles within itself. Both halves are united to form a complete and androgynous human.

Of course, the question naturally arises, how and why did these primordial dyads become separated? We will deal with this question at length in Chapter Two.

Chapters Two, Four, Five, Six and Seven focus directly on the issue of soul mates. But why, you might ask, does this book also deal with the themes of creation, the fall from grace and nirvana? The answer is this: If we want to understand the path of soul mates, we need to begin our inquiry at a point in time prior to their division into two beings so that we can form an idea of their primal state. To accomplish this, we need to discuss the creation, as well as the fall from grace (original sin), which is intimately interwoven with the story of the creation of the visible cosmos and the division of soul mates. This bifurcation not only includes their partition into two beings, but also refers to the spatial separation that often prevents them from finding one another again. Therefore, it behooves us to carefully examine the fall from grace and its consequences. Finally, nirvana is the Eastern term for the primordial state of being in which souls existed before creation and before the fall from grace. Nirvana is also the state to which, sooner or later, depending upon their evolutionary status, those souls will one day return. Nirvana is equivalent to the "Kingdom of God" as preached by Jesus.

I wish my readers much pleasure and many new insights through their study of this book.

12

I. CREATION

From where did creation come? Did He establish it or not,
He who dwells in the highest heaven and who watches
over all? He alone knows the answer; or does even He not
know?

Rig Veda

In very few words, this verse from the Rig Veda's "Song of Creation" expresses just about everything that even the most spiritually advanced human beings really know about creation and its causes—or, rather, it expresses everything that such individuals *do not* and *cannot* know. At this point in our study, we need to focus on two questions: *Why* did creation take place? And from *where* did it come? I shall try my best to answer these questions.

Why was the visible cosmos created in the first place? After all, is not the true home of all souls with God, and are they not surrounded by bodily husks for the duration of the cosmic journey that separates them from God and their original home?

The answer, it seems, can only be that the visible cosmos was created in order to give these souls who had drifted away from God something to hold onto. Before so-called "original sin" took place, the visible cosmos did not exist. Its creation became necessary after some souls turned away from God. Creation of the visible cosmos enabled them to enjoy the illusion of *maya* and to experience the pain of suffering. The pain they suffer, however, should not be construed as an act of divine *revenge*, but as something to impel them to think carefully about their suffering so they can ultimately turn around on their path *away from God* and turn their steps *toward God* once more. There are many reasons to agree with the Buddhist doctrine claiming that there is no God the Creator and that the world is simply the interaction of a myriad of mutually interdependent factors. According to this view, material creation is the result of erroneous behavior by the souls incarnated within the material cosmos. After all, is it not rather difficult to imagine that a God sitting on His throne in heaven would ever feel bored enough to come up with the idea of creating a cosmos simply to help Him while away His idle hours?

This brings us to our second question: From where did the creation of the visible cosmos come?

The answer is that the cosmos was created through the materialization of spiritual thought. Yogananda explains the genesis and essence of the visible cosmos as a dream of God (*maya*). According to his convincing thesis, consciousness is the fundamental stuff of the universe, and matter is merely energy on a coarser plane of manifestation. Yogananda concludes that cosmic energy is no more than a projection of God's will.[1] This opinion is shared by the Indian Brahmins, who teach that this world is rooted in thought (i.e., in consciousness).

According to St. John, creation took place not only through an act of consciousness, or thought, but also by virtue of the Word. We will examine this idea shortly, but first we need to show that consciousness, thought and the Word are actually three interwoven aspects of one and the same reality. Everything begins with consciousness: without it there would be no thought, and without thought there would be no Word. Consciousness is the essential core. When consciousness becomes aware of itself, it begins to think. Thought flows from consciousness and is therefore described as the first emanation. Thought completes and perfects itself in the spoken Word, which is the second emanation of consciousness. However, this second emanation can only be attained with the help of thought as a mediator between consciousness and the Word.

This state of affairs is corroborated in the story of creation as described in The Gospel According to St. John: "In the beginning was the Word, and the Word was with God, and the Word was God." (John 1:1) "The same was in the beginning with God." (John 1:2) "All things were made by Him; and without Him was not anything made." (John 1:3) "In Him was life; and that life was the light of men." (John 1:4) "And the light shineth in darkness; and the darkness comprehendeth it not." (John 1:1-5)

We find striking parallels between John 1:1 and the Rig Veda, in which the complementary feminine principle that expresses God's creative aspect is given the name *Vac*. Vac is the Word and, when Vac speaks, the world is formed. John 1:1 and 1:2 suggest that the nature of God is twofold. On the one hand, having called forth the cosmos from out of Himself, He entered into all of creation and into each individual entity. On the other hand, He rests within Himself in complete contentment, entirely separate from all created forms. The Svetashvatara Upanishad expresses this view: "Only He is the universe, everything that was, everything that ever will be. He became cosmic space, and yet He remains eternally unchangeable."[2]

The Brihadaranyaka Upanishad is yet another of the many scriptures that verify John 1:3. According to this ancient Hindu text, "This Self is Lord and King above all beings. Just as the spokes of a wheel are held together by the hub and the rim, so, too, are all beings, all creatures, all gods, all worlds, all living things held together within the Self. The Self created two-legged creatures and four-legged creatures, then it penetrated into all bodies and began to dwell in the heart of the lotus. One can call it *purusha* [spirit]. Nothing could exist were it not surrounded by, and imbued with, purusha. It took on all forms. It took on all shapes so

that it could manifest itself through their forms. The Self, the Lord, manifests itself through all the many forms of *maya*, becoming tens, thousands and endless myriads."[3]

We can conclude from these scriptures that nothing exists that did not originate from God. Consequently, the figure of the devil in Christianity and of Satan in Islam are not independent entities or powers opposed to God, but rather represent all those entities who chose not to live in harmony with their origin (i.e., with God).

John 1:4 lends further support to the preceding verse by expressly stating that all entities draw their life from the Light (which is equivalent to *spirit*) and that their destiny was, is and always will be to wander and dwell within this illumination (i.e., within the spirit of God). When the emanations of this Light individualized, some mistakenly assumed themselves to be independent entities. Foolishly believing they could exist apart from God, their erroneous notions engendered the darkness within them. In reality, of course, there is no darkness, as John 1:5 plainly declares. What seems like darkness is a consequence of alienation from God, and can only survive when we are unaware of our true origin. This is why it is written that "God divided the light from the darkness." (Genesis 1:4) Commenting on this verse, the Sohar explains: "The rays of light that the Holy One created radiated from one end of the world to the other and then hid themselves. Why? So that the sinners would not be able to enjoy Him."[4] (When we talk about the "creation of light," we should always remember that, strictly speaking, the phrase is misleading since the divine light has always existed and is therefore uncreated and immortal.) The Sohar further teaches that "the separation of light from darkness refers to the era of exile during which the principle of division prevails."[5]

John 1:5 again informs us about the divine origin of each individual. All entities carry a spark of the divine within themselves, but can only experience its presence through inner contemplation. The Upanishads corroborate this teaching. The Chandogya Upanishad, for example, declares: "Only he who has found Brahman in the innermost depths of his own heart is a true knower of Brahman."[6] The Svetashvatara Upanishad teaches a similar doctrine: "In truth, thou art always united with the Lord. But you must *know* it. Nothing else is worth knowing."[7]

John 1:5 also reminds us of the merciless persecution that has been perpetrated by the ignorant masses of humanity upon so many of the great spiritual teachers. There has been, unfortunately, no lack of martyrs, as we realize when we consider the fate suffered by Origenes and Socrates, or when we recall the crucifixion of Jesus. John 1:5 tells us that all of nature and all living creatures (i.e., humans as well as animals) are projections of God and that, by contemplating His creations, we can recognize God. People who languish in the darkness of material creation have not comprehended this truth. In countless ways, they continue to sin against God and His emanations, ignorant of the fact that He can be discovered everywhere. These are the ignorant and destructive people who wage wars against other human beings, who slaughter animals and ravage the natural environment.

At this point I want to emphasize that the stories about the creation of the world that I cited above form the basis of consciousness, thought and the Word. They should not be interpreted as descriptions of a creation *ex nihilo* (out of nothingness). Rather, the process of creation can be understood as a materialization of pre-existent components whose substance is without beginning and without end.

The story of creation recounted by Uddalaka in the Chandogya Upanishad agrees with this, saying: "In the beginning was being—only one, without a second. Some people claim that in the beginning there was nonbeing and that the cosmos arose from that. But how could that be possible? How could being arise from nonbeing? No, my son, in the beginning there was being, nothing besides being—only one, without a second."[8]

The teachings of Origenes support this view and assert the immortality of the primordial substance: "It can take unto itself change and difference and, according to its merits, it will be placed on a higher or a lower level, but dissolution of substance can never be suffered by something that God made to exist and endure." (*de princ.* III,6)

Material creation (i.e., the universe, of which our planet, the sun and the entire visible cosmos are parts) was the final step in a series of events that took place during the period of creation. Long before the material universe arose, like sparks from an infinite light, spiritual beings emanated from God, the Great Spirit. This first emanation was initiated by God; afterwards, material creation resulted when these souls fell from grace, drifted away from God and individuated. The Sohar explains this situation with a parable: "This is the meaning of the words, *A wise son pleases his father, a foolish son grieves his mother.* The wise son is the human being in the state of emanation; the foolish son is the human being in the state of creation."[9]

The various epochs of creation proceed concentrically from within to without. Emanation is also sometimes represented as moving from above to below—that is, from the most ethereal to the most material—and, thus, from the primal spirit toward the final stage of materialized creation. Many stories and myths about creation agree that it occurred through emanation and extension. The form of the human being itself clearly shows that creation must have proceeded in this manner. Jesus said, "The kingdom of heaven is within you." And Buddha warned: "If you meet a Buddha on the road, kill him, because he is a false Buddha. The true Buddha is within you." Hidden deep within our innermost being, in our central core, so to speak, lies the divine spark, the Self. This spark is surrounded by the soul, which, in turn, is clothed by increasingly denser, more material bodies. These ethereal forms incarnate in material bodies here on Earth or elsewhere. The whole of creation proceeds according to this same pattern: at the core we find God, who is eternal, who rests within Himself, who never changes, yet who simultaneously permeates all beings. Redeemed beings who have returned to their original state (nirvana) can be construed as dwelling close to (or within) this divine center. The core of this inner circle does not change; it is exempt from time, suffering, birth and death. Entities who dwell here enjoy everlasting, ultimate bliss.

The next concentric circle is an intermediate stage between the inner and outer circle. A soul who has reached this stage exists in an intermediate state of being in which it passes the interval between earthly or other material incarnations. It refreshes itself here, rethinks its past incarnation and prepares itself for its next venture into a material body. Here, as among the redeemed beings in the divine center, there is no sense of time.

The outermost circle is comprised of souls who have entered into material incarnation. The wheel of time whirls here. According to the Svetashvatara Upanishad: "The vast expanse of space is an eternally turning wheel, the wheel of Brahman. All creatures who are subject to birth, death and rebirth are bound to this wheel. For as long as individual entities continue to believe that they are separate from Brahman, they must continue to turn upon the wheel, subject to the law of death and rebirth. But when, through Brahman's grace, an entity realizes its oneness with Him, it need no longer turn together with the wheel. It has attained immortality."[10]

From the literature cited above, we can see that time is only a relative concept and, as such, exists only in the coarser, material realm. Plato expresses a similar view in his *Timaeus*, in which he explains that the concept of time cannot be applied to the realm of immortal being, since only the unchanging present exists in that realm (*Timaeus 29a*). In his book *Sphärenwanderer* (*Wanderer Through the Spheres*), Herbert Engel describes the process of creation as occurring together with the onset of time: "Space arose when the primordial energy moved out of oneness and into the first manifestation of dynamic tension. The primal point of concentration rested within itself. But a second one immediately began to orbit about the first one. And thus time began."[11] The various worlds become progressively less pure as we descend the rungs of this cosmic ladder. Our material world is the lowest and, thus, least pure realm of all.[12]

From the literature just cited, we can readily understand that the material cosmos is, in fact, nothing other than a (albeit severely distorted) reflection of higher spiritual spheres. People conversant with the spiritual world teach the fundamental equivalence of *above* and *below*. Each visible form is a reflection of an eternal idea, since, without a prior model, no corresponding depiction could exist. All of these forms have dispersed outward, from the interior toward the exterior. Timaeus, in section 29a of Plato's dialogue of the same name, explains that the created world is a depiction based on a prior model: "If this world is beautiful and its author good, then His gaze must have been fixed upon that which is immortal. It is heretical to suggest that He based creation upon something that was already created."

Yet another question arises in connection with creation: Was creation a one-time-only process or does it repeat itself in unceasing cycles? Some religions teach the cyclical doctrine, an opinion that was shared by Origenes. Hindu theories of cyclical creation assert that the universe exists while Brahman (the Creator) is awake, and continues to exist—from its creation until its destruction—only as long as Brahman remains awake. When Brahman falls asleep, the cosmos returns to its primal element, the so-called "original atom." One widely accepted Western scientific model likewise assumes that the universe was created in an instantaneous "big bang" and has been expanding ever since. After it reaches its point of greatest expansion, a subsequent phase of contraction will begin, and the universe will start to shrink back toward the dimensionless point from which it began.

Helena P. Blavatsky states that there is an infinite being who exists eternally, and who is alternately passive or active. During its active periods, the divine entity expands until, as its final act, it brings forth the visible universe. During its passive periods, the divine being withdraws into itself, and all material entities in the physical universe pass out of existence.[13]

The Koran also describes a cyclical process of creation. Sura 29:20 contains the words: "See they not how God bringeth forth creation and then causeth it to return again?"

It would be erroneous, however, to conclude that the whole cosmos has been created and destroyed many times. We know that entire solar systems are born and others die within this gigantic cosmos, so a cyclical process obviously exists within the universe. But this alone neither proves nor disproves the theory that the entire cosmos *as a whole* is subject to cycles of creation and dissolution. According to Helena P. Blavatsky: "The secret doctrines about the evolution of the entire cosmos cannot be conveyed because they cannot be understood, even by the most advanced minds of this age."[14]

I personally believe that the entire cosmos could perhaps be subject to repeated cycles of creation and destruction for a certain period of time. For this hypothesis to be correct, there must have been a beginning and, since there was a beginning, there would also have to be an end. The basis for my belief is that, as we saw earlier, the material world arose only in order to provide fallen entities with something to which they could cling. Consequently, the creation of additional material worlds would only occur if it were necessary for the further evolution and spiritual redemption of entities who had fallen away from God. When the last entity is finally redeemed, all further material creation will be superfluous. If, on the other hand, we were to claim that the cycles of material creation and dissolution continue without end, we would deny all those doctrines that maintain that, at some point, the soul permanently reunites with its origin. We would deny a teaching ascribed to no lesser an authority than the Buddha himself, who taught: "For him who has attained nirvana, there is no return to this world." Furthermore, if it were true that material creation took place in order to provide fallen beings with something to which they could cling, assuming that creation continues in endless cycles would lead to the nonsensical conclusion that God does not reign over all cosmic processes and that, ultimately, everything returns to chaos all over again.

The cosmic, primordial egg plays an important role in many myths of creation. This ultimate ovum is often related not only to the macrocosmos, but also to the microcosmos—that is, the creation of human beings. Myths about this subject serve as an excellent transition to our next chapter, in which we will learn about the division of the originally androgynous human being into male and female halves.

In a Hindu poem about creation, it is said that the golden egg grew from a seed that floated upon the cosmic ocean for an entire year. Finally, Brahman hatched from that egg and divided into two entities, one male and one female. The Indian concept of *purusha* is likewise related to a myth about the binary division of a cosmic egg. In that story, however, the female element issues from the male half. This ancient tale provides us with yet another hint that the state of primal androgyny applies to the entire cosmos as well as to each individual person. The binary division into spirit and matter, as well as the division into male and female, apply to everything in nature.

According to a creation myth told by the Kaiva Kamu clan in the village of Orokolo, near the Gulf of Papua, the first pair of human beings hatched from an egg. At this time, the surface of the Earth was entirely covered by water. Nothing lived in this watery world except one huge tortoise, who used her mighty, webbed limbs to scoop up land from the bottom of the ocean. This mass of land grew larger amd larger, until the tortoise finally crawled onto it and rested there. After she had rested, she began to dig holes in the ground. Each of these holes was larger than a house, and into these holes she laid her eggs. After some time, the first human beings hatched from these eggs. The first people to emerge from the tortoise eggs were named Ivi Apo and Kerema Apo. According to the lore of the Kaiva Kamu, these two people were the first human couple. But, at this primordial time, Ivi Apo and Kerema Apo were not yet male or female because they did not have sexual organs. Their loins were smooth and featureless. Only later did Kerema Apo become a man and Ivi Apo become a woman.

24

2. ᴅɪⱯɪꟻɪọN

Together with Chapters Five and Seven, this chapter about the binary division of the originally androgynous human being into two separate beings, a man and a woman, forms the focal point of this book. Here, in Chapter Two, we will see that this theme is discussed not only in Plato's *Symposium*, but, because it is archetypal wisdom, is also present within every great religious tradition and in the myths of many aboriginal peoples throughout the world.

To be systematic amid the diversity of information presented, we will compare individual tales with one another. This will allow us to see where they agree and where they seem to be contradictory. Relevant verses from Genesis will be used as a benchmark for these comparisons. Each biblical excerpt will be given extensive commentary and will be compared with other traditional stories.

Let us then begin by considering the relevant verses in Genesis.

So God created man in His own image; in the image of
God, created He him; male and female, created He them.
(1:27)

According to Edgar Cayce, in the beginning, when souls were first created, they were neither male nor female, but both—a complete whole.

Simon Magus teaches that, when God formed the first human being by gathering dust from the Earth, He did not form the primal human as a single, simple entity. Instead, God fashioned the primal human as a double being, according to His image.

In the Sohar, we read that the human being of the emanation was male and female at the same time. Thus, the human being at this stage had two faces. Only this figure truly deserves to be called a human being.

Dozens of other myths tell of an originally androgynous (i.e., double-gendered, male-female) entity that later divided into male and female parts. It is clear, then, that in the events described in the first chapter of Genesis, God created the human being as a man and a woman, (i.e., as a male-female entity). As a consequence of this primal divine emanation, a complete, whole, male-female entity arose out of God. Only later, in another stage of creation, did this holistic entity become divided (or divide itself) into two parts, into the polarity of male and female. This division was probably related to the fall into the material realm, since everything here in the material world is composed of polarities (e.g., day and night, life and death, beginning and end, health and sickness). The human being, who likewise dwells within the material realm, and whose earthly body arose from matter, cannot escape these dualities and is subject to the laws of polarity. We should note that the separation of genders was related to the fall into matter, and that the original human being on Earth was still androgynous, as various myths tell us. The primal human did not separate into two genders until a later point in time. Hermann Rudolph explains this apparent contradiction as follows: "The separation of the androgynous human beings into men and women occurred in the middle of the third, or Lemurian, race (eighteen million years ago) when evolution had reached the lowest stage and the physical body had attained its complete formation and density. This concluded the process of declining into matter."[1]

To sum up, we can see that our conclusions agree with what St. Paul writes in his first epistle to the Corinthians (11:12): "For

as the woman is of the man, even so is the man also by the woman;
but all things are of God." Edgar Cayce concurs: "Thanks to
their androgynous divine nature, the first souls were able to create a *companion self* by an act of will, splitting that companion
off from themselves."[2] Only the creature described in Genesis 1
is the complete image of God; the human being in Genesis 2 is
whole only when considered together with its opposite pole (i.e.,
the man becomes whole through the woman, and vice versa).

At this point I will briefly discuss the difficulties of bringing the
first three chapters of Genesis into a mutually noncontradictory
context. On the one hand, they ought to be, at least in part, interpreted chronologically. On the other hand, when we try to interpret
them in a strictly chronological fashion, they prove to be too contradictory to support such an endeavor. For example, although the
first chapter of Genesis describes the creation of the Earth and its
inhabitants (both the beasts and the male-female human, who is
quite obviously still androgynous), we need not assume that this
was necessarily a material creation. It is entirely possible that the
created world described here was an ethereal realm, a world of
immaterial forms that later served as the model upon which the
materialized forms were based. Further support for this hypothesis
can be found in Genesis 2:7. Only at this point, in the second chapter of Genesis, was a human being sculpted from the dust of the
earth and the breath of life first breathed into its nostrils.

The supposition that the subsequent separation of the human
being into male and female halves actually took place in a materialized body is difficult to conceive. The division of soul mates
is a splitting apart, and this split occurs in an ethereal body, not
a material one. The descriptions found in many traditional stories might lead us to believe that the division occurred in matter,
but these tales ought to be understood in a more profoundly
mystical, allegorical sense related to another plane of being. The
chronology described in the Bible suggests that, after soul mates
were divided so that they could serve as companions for one
another, and were given the paradisiacal garden—which never

existed on Earth, but is located in the astral realm—to dwell in, they were exiled to this planet as a result of their own error. (We will discuss this in depth in the following chapter.)

Although the actual path of soul mates within the material world is not described until the fourth chapter of Genesis, verse 3:23 clearly states: "God sent him forth from the garden of Eden to till the ground *from whence he was taken*." This phrase contains apparent contradictions that I am unable to explain as fully as I might wish. You should understand that some verses describe events in the astral realm that seem to contradict events occurring in the material realm. Certain biblical verses apparently describe several planes of being simultaneously and, as we said before, the various chapters of the Bible are not arranged in strict chronological order. For example, we know that the first chapter of Genesis was written in the sixth century B.C. by a Jewish priest and that the second chapter (beginning with verse 2:4) was composed by a poet who lived in Jerusalem during the nineth century B.C. For this reason, the first chapter of Genesis is described as the priestly story of creation (P) and the second chapter as the Yahwistic story of creation (Y).

But let us return to our main theme. Rudolf Passian writes as follows about soul mates: "According to the doctrine of soul mates, we human beings originally came into being as pure spirits. Every 'I' was accompanied by a 'Thou,' and together they formed a unique, self-complementary, energetically fluid unity."[3]

Helena P. Blavatsky describes the original androgyny of the primal human being: "Every nation considered its first God or gods to be androgynous; and it could not be otherwise, since they regarded their remote original progenitors, their doubly sexed ancestors, as divine entities and gods."[4]

A Hebrew myth tells the story of Tebel, the uppermost Earth in a seven-stage construction, on top of which a paradisiacal state reigned. According to this legend, Tebel was inhabited by creatures with double heads. They had "four ears and four eyes, double noses and double mouths, four hands and four legs, but only a single torso. When they sat, they looked like two people, but when they walked, they looked like one person. When they ate and drank, their two heads argued with one another and accused each other of having taken more food or drink than was their own fair share. Nonetheless, they were considered to be righteous beings."[5]

This tale of two-headed human beings is similar to the account given in Plato's *Symposium*, in which he writes that there were originally three genders: a female, a male and a male-female. This, of course, is not strictly true since man and woman came from the division of a male-female entity. In this otherwise highly informative work, Plato cites a speech by Aristophanes to the effect that there were originally three genders and that the male-male and female-female genders were likewise separated—namely, into two men or two women. This is an erroneous assumption since all souls were originally identical. Plato's theory is an attempt to explain the origin of homosexuality, but there must be other reasons behind it as well. For example, two souls who have incarnated into bodies of the same gender instinctively know that their dual soul has also taken on the same gender in this present incarnation. Alternately, because one soul incarnated in the opposite gender for many past incarnations, it cannot fully identify itself with its present gender role.

This is what Aristophanes has to say about the male-female gender in *Symposium:* "For at that time one race was androgynous, and in looks and name it combined both the male as well as the female." Further on we read: "The looks of each human being were as a whole round, with back and sides in a circle. And each had four arms, and legs equal in number to the arms, and two faces alike in all respects on a cylindrical neck, but there was one head for both faces—they were set in opposite directions—and four ears, and two sets of genitals and all the rest that one might conjecture from this."

The Aztec creation saga of Teztcoco tells of a similarly intimate relationship between man and woman: "Early one morning, the sun god shot an arrow down from heaven...Out of the hole pierced by this arrow, there came forth a man and a woman...The man's body existed only from the armpits upward, the woman's body likewise, and in order to breed children the man would thrust his tongue into the mouth of the woman. Like magpies or sparrows, they moved forward only by hopping."[6] Another Aztec legend about a gemstone bone composed partly from the bones of men and partly from the bones of women, as well as a myth from the Solomon Islands—according to which a cane of sugar produced two buds out of which sprouted a man and a woman—hint at the common origins and intimate linkage between man and woman.

Corroboration for this view is found in the mythology of the Jaina sect in India. These people believe in the existence of an earlier epoch when "man and woman were born together as twins. Each had 64 ribs and was two miles tall."[7] It is not known for certain, but it seems likely that this is the meaning to be construed from verse 8:44 of the Hebrew Adam script, in which it is written: "Before Chavah (i.e., Eve) died, and in accordance with marital rites performed with the utmost holiness and honor, she bore thirty pairs of twins, each of which was composed of one son and one daughter."[8]

In the Hindu tradition and in certain tantric Buddhist tales, we find further evidence of the originally androgynous nature of every entity, although this androgyny is not directly related to the human realm. For example, the Katha Upanishad says: "Prajapati was this universe. Vac was his helpmate. He joined with her... she bore living creatures and then returned back into Prajapati."[9] Shiva, who is widely worshipped (especially in southern India) and his consort Shakti together form "the first and original unfolding of Brahman in the polarities of the male and female principles."[10] At the same time, Shiva is endowed with human attributes, since it is said that he finds his earthly counterpart in every mortal man, just as Shakti finds her counterpart in every mortal woman.[11]

Some readers may have difficulty comprehending the fact that humankind was originally hermaphroditic (i.e., doubly sexed), since at first glance it would seem that no androgynous life forms exist on Earth. Closer study of biology, however, reveals that hermaphroditism is still quite common among a wide range of smaller-sized, invertebrate animals.

> *And the Lord God said, "It is not good that the man*
> *should be alone; I will make him an help meet for him."*
> *(2:18)*

Almost without a gap, this verse follows from Genesis 1:27. The complete human being was still a male-female double entity, but was lonesome and yearned for companionship. Nearly all the world's great religions agree on this. Buddhism is the sole exception, not because it contradicts this, but simply because it does not deal with this issue at all. The same process of primal division can be found in many different myths, in the dialogues of Plato and in the writings of Edgar Cayce. Opinions differ, however, about whether this originally androgynous being was divided by God (as the Bible, Koran and Plato teach) or whether it divided itself (as is reported by the Eastern traditions and by Edgar Cayce). Regardless of who did the splitting, the fact remains that the Bible, Hindu sources and Edgar Cayce all agree upon the loneliness of that primal hermaphrodite as the motive for the division. On the other hand, some traditional accounts view the division of the primal double entity as a punishment. This is the opinion expressed, for example, in Plato's *Symposium* and in certain gnostic texts.

Our examination of these cases leads us to ask whether the various traditional accounts are contradictory or whether closer study might reveal that the apparent contradictions could be reconciled or interpreted in a way that would make them complementary. As far as the cause of this binary division is concerned, we know that God created humankind (or that the souls emanated from God). Since these souls bear all attributes of God within themselves (although nowadays only intuitively and unconsciously), they are regarded as embodying the divine image. Thus, there is no contradiction between the tradition that claims the separation into man and woman was brought about by God and the tradition that maintains that the originally androgynous human being became man and woman through self-division. Neither are the reasons for this division necessarily contradictory since the division of an androgynous entity into two beings of opposite genders could have been motivated by the loneliness of that primordial hermaphrodite and its desire for a companion. The notion of separation as a punishment, then, need not refer to the aforementioned division into two beings of opposite genders, but can be interpreted as referring to the subsequent *spatial* separation of those single-gendered creatures. This latter separation of soul partners, whom we describe as "soul mates," is the punishment inflicted upon them for having committed a misdeed. It is for this reason that they are prevented from encountering one another throughout many long incarnations.

According to gnostic philosophers, "the existence of woman is a permanent reminder of the primal division....The division is viewed as the destruction of a perfect world, but gnosis offers us the potential to overcome this split and reestablish the unity of paradise: Eve can once again be subsumed within Adam."[12]

In the Sohar we find the following description of the division of the original human into man and woman. Rabbi Acha begins with this account from the First Book of Moses: "And JHWH Elohim [Yahweh or God the Lord] said, 'It is not good that the man should be alone.'" Why does He begin with these words? It is taught that the reason for this is the same as the reason God

did not complete His second day's work with the words, 'And
God saw that it was good': because it was on this day that the
human being first felt lonesome. But was that primal human really lonely? After all, it is said that 'male and female, He created
them.' And we have learned that the human being was created
with two faces, and God said that 'it is not good that the man
should be alone.' But that primal human ignored the female component and did not rely upon it, since only the male side was
formed and, from the back, they looked like one—thus, the primal human was alone. 'I will make him a helpmate for him.'
(Genesis 2:18) This means a helpmate who can face him, so that
each can help the other, face-to-face. What did the Holy One
do? He cut the primal human in half with a saw and took the
female portion from him. It is written, 'and he took one of his
ribs.' (Genesis 2:21) What does 'one' mean here? It means his
feminine side, in the same sense as in the words 'My dove, my
undefiled, is but one.' (Song of Songs 6:9) 'And He brought her
to Adam.' (Genesis 2:22) He adorned her like a bride and led her
to appear before his shining face: face-to-face."[13]

This account is clearly allegorical and should certainly not be
taken literally. This fact becomes particularly obvious when we
realize that God surely did not use a saw to separate the female
part from the male part. But, if we read and interpret it correctly,
this text can shed light on some profound mysteries.

At this point, we should ask just how the division of the genders ought to be understood in the first place. If man and woman
are really two poles of the same primal individual, two halves of
a primordial hermaphrodite who was subsequently split asunder, it ought to be the case that they are quite literally "made for
one another," to be each other's companions. But, since they
have become two entities, they must have already been two—
or, at least, have possessed the latent capacity to become two—
before their division. (See Chapter Seven, in which I describe
the union of astral bodies that serves as the higher model for the
sexual union of two lovers who are incarnated in material bod-

ies.) If, on the other hand, they were already two distinct entities—who could merge into one at any time, or separate from one another to again become two—then they obviously were not yet aware of the binary division chronicled in Genesis 2:21ff. Each experienced itself as alone and lonesome because neither could recognize the existence of its companion.

Further support for this assumption can be found in various legends (e.g., Plato's *Symposium*) in which it is said that the two halves of the primal hermaphrodite were bound together *back-to-back*. This allegorical formulation is trying to tell us that both components were already present (as two parts), but did not yet have any knowledge of each other's existence. This explains why they felt so lonely and without support. Their subsequent presentation to one another *face-to-face* means that in the instant of this encounter they confronted one another, became consciously aware of each other and realized that they are in fact two halves of the same being. (Genesis expresses this realization in Adam's words: "This is now...flesh of my flesh.") From this moment on, they provide each other with mutual assistance and support ("I will make him a helpmate for him"). The creation of woman as described here is not really a division of the primal hermaphrodite, but merely the conscious recognition of its feminine part.

Before it became conscious of its feminine aspect (Genesis 2:23), the primal human being was in a state of profound slumber. (Genesis 2:21) That is, it was unaware of the fact that a companion was already present but as of yet unacknowledged. The Brihadaranyaka Upanishad, for example, reports that while we can only see and know another in duality, for an enlightened one the universe dissolves into itself. This verse closes by asking two related questions: Who is seen by whom? And who ought to recognize whom? Since the Brihadaranyaka Upanishad describes a desirable situation that obviously refers to nirvana (the final state of all souls and the state of being in which they found themselves at the beginning), it naturally lends support to our thesis. However, it also raises two additional questions that will be left unanswered here: Why are the loneliness and the unawareness of the other that are associated with that loneliness viewed as desirable states of being? And, if this description is meant to be taken literally, would recognition of the woman's existence be a negative development, since all duality began with that recognition?

To sum up, we can conclude that the binary division as described in the second chapter of Genesis made man aware of his already existent other half and that the two parts ultimately recognized one another. As we have already briefly mentioned (and as we will discuss in more detail later on), the process can also occur in the opposite direction. In other words, soul mates can—and should—find their way back to their primordial, essential unity. However, in this reunification they remain two entities, since neither is ever lost or negated. Whether their union involves the merging of soul mates into one another, or the union of each soul with all other redeemed souls and with the ultimate substance of life (generally referred to as God) in nirvana, that unification does not involve the loss of identity. Consequently, prior to the binary division, the soul mates must already have existed as two distinct entities who were ignorant of each other's existence. Together, yet unaware of each other, each pair formed a unified, primordial and complete human being.

At this point in our discussion, we need only note what the aforementioned biblical verse expressly states—and must mean allegorically—namely, that a man or woman only becomes a genuine human being when he or she acknowledges his or her opposite pole. A man becomes fully male through his recognition of the feminine within him, and a woman becomes fully female through her recognition of the masculine within her.

And the Lord God caused a deep sleep to fall upon Adam,
and he slept: and He took one of his ribs, and closed up
the flesh instead thereof. (2:21)

This verse, in which the originally androgynous human being becomes two entities during deep sleep, or during a period of profound unconsciousness, means that both entities were already together as a single being. However, because of their fall into the dualism of the material realm, they become subject to polarity and thus had to be separated into two genders. Bearing in mind the hypothesis presented above, the division they are subjected to during this deep sleep or deep unconsciousness either means that both halves (the male as well as the female) were languishing in a deep spiritual sleep until the moment they *recognized* (Genesis 2:23) each other as soul companions, or else it means that neither half was capable of remembering the other. We have all experienced the phenomenon of *not remembering*: for example, we frequently wake up in the morning unable to recall the previous night's dreams (or astral journeys). Most of us are similarly incapable of remembering the time before our births (e.g., the time we spent in our mothers' wombs, our previous incarnations). In many cases, the perpetrator, or even the victim, of an evil or shameful deed is unable to recall the event because the memory has been lost or repressed. Similarly, it is quite possible that the divided human being can no longer recall the reason for, and the actual execution of, that division. The subsequent recognition ("This is now...flesh of my flesh") corresponds to the startling intuition that sometimes brightens our lives when we "fall in love at first sight."

The phenomenon of love at first sight usually involves recognition of a soul whom we loved greatly during a previous incarnation. Spontaneous feelings of affection or dislike for people whom we have never met before during this lifetime are likewise based on encounters that took place during previous incarnations. When we meet such individuals, we immediately experience either a pleasant feeling of well-being or an uneasy sense of apprehension. The individuals who catalyze these feelings need not be the actual people who merit these reactions, but may simply remind us of those people through similarities of physical appearance or through shared character traits.

The motif of a deep sleep during which the primal human is given a soul companion is also found among the Quiche, according to whom the first human beings were four men. "They are called 'made' [rather than 'born'] because they had neither mothers nor fathers, and they are simply called 'humans.' No woman gave birth to them, nor were they engendered by the Creator; they were created by Him entirely by magical means....During a sleep they were given truly beautiful wives.... And immediately their hearts were glad because now they had mates."[14]

Both the Quiche story and the biblical report of a "deep sleep" might lead us to believe that the primal human "dreamed up" a companion. If, for the moment, we ignore the previously discussed possibility that Adam merely became aware of his female other half, then we could readily interpret the biblical and Quiche accounts to mean that the man dreamed a woman for himself. If this were true, the soul companion would be nothing more than a "figment of our imagination." But, since the soul mate was created during a profound slumber, it cannot be the product of a deliberate, conscious conception, but must have been engendered unconsciously from the heartfelt yearning to have a commensurate companion, to no longer be alone and to have a helper for our life's labors.

When the holistic being first materialized, it incarnated in an androgynous (astral) body. This body was engendered purely by energy and was not gestated within a physical womb. It was alone and longed for an appropriate companion, but its mate could only be created from the primordial hermaphrodite itself, because only with such a partner could a genuine relationship develop. The desire for companionship became so strong that, with God's help and by virtue of its own spiritual power, it assumed a material form. The first being, generally referred to as "man" (although in my view it would be more appropriate to speak of two intimately interwoven halves), fell asleep. When he awoke (we are following the traditional story and using male pronouns, although it would be equally correct to describe the process with feminine pronouns), he saw a beautiful female (or she saw a handsome male) creature lying beside him (or her). This mate had arisen from the original hermaphrodite, either as a materialization of its spiritual yearning or as the self-division and recognition of a previously unacknowledged other half. We should not mistakenly assume that this process merely involves the creation of one physical body from another. In that case, it would be much like that of a newborn baby which should be regarded as a spiritual excrescence of its mother, but which fully deserves to be recognized as an independent individual with its own biography and its own karma based on its previous existence. Rather, the relationship between soul mates derives from the fact that both are formed from one and the same spiritual entity.

And the rib, which the Lord God had taken from man,
made He a woman, and brought her unto the man. (2:22)

The Bible is quite clear that the materials for the creation of the woman were taken from the man (or, rather, from the holistic human) and not from anywhere else. Man and woman are thus dependent upon one another. Mutually and ideally complementary, they are two halves of a whole—two halves of the same person. The creation of Eve from Adam's rib, or from his side, suggests that we are not dealing with the creation of something entirely new, but are witnessing the splitting of a preexisting entity so that woman (and man) can begin to exist independently.

According to Luther, the Hebrew word *zela* can be translated both as "rib" and as "side." When we consider that man and woman arose through the division of the originally androgynous

human being, "side" seems to be the more appropriate translation. Helena P. Blavatsky agrees with this interpretation: "Eva was not conceived, she was drawn out of Adam in much the same way that amoeba A cinches itself together in the middle and splits in half to yield amoeba B—through division."[15]

After the woman was formed from his rib—or, to be more precise, was taken from his side— she is shown to him. But she is not taken from just anywhere, from some arbitrary external location, and then shown to him: instead, she is made from his own component parts. Thus, we can see that two people whom God has made for one another arise from a single essential entity—unless karma decrees otherwise, which is the case in many incarnations. In the same way, all androgynous entities arise from the one great being—namely, from God.

Another "rib version" is found in the mythology of the Cheyenne Indians. According to this traditional tale, man was formed from a rib taken from the Highest Being, and then woman was formed from a rib taken from the man.[16] In analyzing this myth, the second phase of which is identical with the biblical description of the creation of woman, we must avoid falling prey to the error of exoteric interpretation and concluding that, since woman was taken from man, man must be older and, thus, more valuable. The truth is that the biblical version of the tale recounts the division of an originally androgynous being into a male and a female part, or else describes a process by which two different halves belonging to the same individual each became aware of their own and each other's existence. We find corroboration for this view in the following statements.

St. Paul, who interprets the tale of woman's creation from Adam's rib literally, errs in his first epistle to the Corinthians when he writes: "For the man is not of the woman; but the woman of the man. Neither was the man created for the woman; but the woman for the man." (First Corinthians 11:8-9) Afterward he corrects himself and writes: "Nevertheless, neither is the man without the woman, neither the woman without the man, in the Lord. For as the woman is of the man, even so is the man also by the woman; but all things of God." (First Corinthians 11:11-12)

Wilhelm Kienzler writes that "the authoritative Hebrew version does not speak of a rib taken from Adam, but says that God took the woman 'from Adam's side.' In other words, God divided androgynous Adam into two separate entities, into man and woman."[17] As we have already explained in our commentary on Genesis 2:22, the Hebrew word *zela* can be translated both as "rib" and as "side." The meaning that the author of this biblical passage is trying to convey is best expressed when *zela* is understood to mean "side." This is one case in which we can readily see how a faulty translation can distort the meaning of the original text.

The view taken in Plato's *Symposium* is echoed in a Hebrew myth that says: "Adam was originally created as a hermaphrodite with a male and a female body, the two bodies being conjoined back-to-back. Since this position made both locomotion and communication difficult, God severed the hermaphrodite into two halves and gave each half its own backside."[18] The Sohar also devotes attention to this theme: "The feminine is inseparable from the realm of the masculine and is thus called 'my dove, my undefiled.' But this should be understood as 'my twin' rather than as 'my undefiled'....When the two unite with one another face-to-face, they truly look like a single body. Consequently, the male alone looks like a mere half body...and likewise the female; only when they join do they become a unity."[19] This passage is especially significant because it uses the word "my twin," a choice of words that clearly confirms the truth of the doctrine of soul mates.

In the Brihadaranyaka Upanishad, we find the following passage that describes separation both on the larger scale (the genesis of the material cosmos) and on the smaller scale (by which the originally androgynous human splits into male and female):

"In the beginning there was only the Self [i.e., the primal One entirely alone]. It was like a human [i.e., an indication of the fundamental equality between the 'small' or microcosmic and the 'large' or macrocosmic human, as well as an indication that humankind was indeed created in God's image]. It looked around and saw nothing other than itself." This passage echoes a commentary by Leo Schaya, who says that when we consider the "One without a second," all of creation takes on the deceptive appearance of a "second." According to Schaya, "Creation is that deceptive 'other' that is really nothing but the 'One without another.' The illusion of the 'other' arises when the One makes itself into its own object; that is, makes itself into an other."[20] The Upanishad continues: "It felt no joy. [In this context, we should recall the similarly unhappy state described in Genesis 2:18]. It wished for a second one. It was as large as a man and a woman embracing one another. It allowed itself to fall asunder into two parts. Thus arose husband and wife. *And therefore*, Yajnavalkya said, *each of us here is like a mere half*."[21]

41

The Koran also informs us about the division of a primal entity into man and woman: "Moreover, God created you of dust—then of the germs of life—then made you two genders." (Sura 35:12) "He created you all of one man, from whom He afterward formed your wife." (Sura 39:7)

And Adam said, This is now bone of my bones, and flesh of my flesh: she shall be called Woman, because she was taken out of Man. (2:23)

In English, it is readily apparent that the words "woman" and "female" are derived from their male counterparts: "wo-man" and "fe-male." This biblical play on words, which is so apparent in English, is difficult to render in German, although Luther's *Männin* is an attempt to emphasize the intimacy of the relationship between Adam and Eve. According to Luther's German translation of the Bible, Eve is called a *Männin*, a word coined by inflecting the vowel and affixing a feminine suffix to *Mann*, the German word for "man." Other German translations describe Eve simply as a *Frau*, the German word for "woman."

Just as every person is intimately aware of his or her own thoughts so, too, Adam and Eve must have immediately recognized the product of their own thoughts—or, because of the essential equality between them, each must have immediately recognized the other as his or her other half. When Adam awoke from his divinely induced slumber, he recognized the woman lying beside him. She was unquestionably the most beautiful creature he had ever seen. He knew right away that she was his soul companion and that both he and she, although separated, were made for one another and belonged together. Their essential kinship is emphasized by the similarity between their names ("man" and "woman") and by the fact that, in many myths, the first human couple bear similar names. It seems appropriate to me to insert a brief digression here.

First of all, we should bear in mind that Adam and Eve—who, in our culture, are generally regarded as the first human beings—are, in fact, synonyms for the first human couple or the first humans. The Hebrew word *Adam* means simply "the human being" and *Eve* or *Eva* translates as "the life." The Kabbala alludes to people who appeared prior to Adam and Eve, know as Hadar and his wife, primal entities who appeared here below and unified spirit and matter in a harmonious but not final form. If Adam and Eve were actually the first human beings, as the Bible's exoteric commentators would have us believe, Cain would never have been able to find his wife in the land of Nod east of Eden. (Genesis 4:16-17) Her presence there proves that there must have been other early races of humans, not solely one first pair of humans. We will find further evidence of this fact later, in subsequent texts. In many tribal languages, the first man and first woman, as well as the male and female parts of the original pair, bear similar names. In some traditions, these first people are described as identical in appearance. In the Persian tradition, for example, the first people were named Meschia and Meschiane and were identical in appearance. The Ceramese call the first people Tuwalamai and Tuwalesi. The Wa name them Yatawm and Yatai. The Japanese call them Izanami and Izanagi.

There could not have been only one first pair of humans, simply because it is difficult to imagine how one pair of parents could have given birth to all the many races found on Earth today. The so-called "first people" must have existed in each of these various places, and subsequent generations must fruitfully (and physically) have multiplied themselves in those places. Additional corroboration of this comes from the fact that *á-dam* is the Sumerian word for "a group of people."

The initial experience of the man, after waking from his divinely induced slumber, during which the primordial human was divided into two entities of different genders, might have been something like this: When he opened his eyes, he found an enchantingly beautiful woman lying close beside him. He immediately recognized her as a part of himself and, in joyful ecstasy, cried, "But you are me!" "Yes, I am indeed you," she no doubt replied, affirming his outburst with a friendly smile that added to his joy. "I am an inseparable part of you," she would have continued, "because I was taken from you." While the man lay there in astonishment, trying to comprehend what had happened during his slumber, she would have continued: "I am a product of your spirit, just as you are a product of the Great Spirit. Didn't you dream about me last night?" "Oh, yes!" he would suddenly have recalled. He had indeed dreamed about a marvelous being who lay beside him.

Thus, the first man created a soul companion for himself out of his own spirit. His yearning for her was so strong that his wish manifested itself in this way. An unprecedented feeling of joy rose within him, filling his entire body and soul.

Hans W. Wolff describes the process as follows: "The unique way in which woman belongs to man is emphasized by the fact that she was not created from the dust of the earth, but from man's own rib, which Yahweh then built into a complete woman. The man, whom God had caused to fall into a profound slumber, was not a witness to the creation of woman. He rejoices when he sees the completed work and recognizes it [her] as being intimately akin to him.[22]

Adam's ecstatic reaction, described above, is comparable to a joyful episode in the Japanese myth of Izanami and Izanagi, the first purely human ancestors. The two of them separate from one another in order to circumambulate the glorious heavenly pillar (the cosmic navel, or post, that links Heaven and Earth) in opposite directions, then encounter one another again on the other side. When they meet, Izanami cries, "Oh, what a handsome man!" and Izanagi exclaims, "Oh, what a beautiful woman!"[23]

Since Adam's and Eve's souls both resounded with the same fundamental harmony, from that moment on, Adam had the companion who was most appropriate for him. In Eve, he finally found the counterpart for whom he had always yearned. He clung to her just as she clung to him, and both enjoyed perfect happiness. Whenever she was out of his sight, he immediately missed her and became painfully aware of how small and incomplete he was without her. She felt the same about him. Neither of them could bear to think they might someday be separated. Their fear was great, but they really had no cause for alarm since God had created them for one another out of a single being with the intention that they remain together. The reason their paths later led them apart, and that they fell away from God (the source of their being), lay in their own misbehavior.

The Koran agrees with this view and relates it to the entirety of humankind: "Men were of one religion only; then they fell to variance." (Sura 10:20)

A mirror, or the reflection in a mirror, is frequently used as a symbol for the intimate link between soul companions. Although their separation into two discrete bodies makes them look like two entities, soul mates are in fact a single spiritual entity. Confirmation of this is found in the writings of Ramala, who says: "Marriage can be compared to a mirror that ever and again confronts both partners with the essence of the creative energy that stands opposite their own."[24] Barry and Joyce Vissell write: "The more deeply a couple love one another, the more perfectly each serves as a mirror for the other."[25]

In our culture, Narcissus is the best-known person to fall in love with his own mirror-image. Narcissus was the son of the Boeotian river Cephissus and the nymph Leiriope. "When Narcissus was a small boy, his mother asked the seer Tiresias whether her son would have a long life. The answer was, 'Yes, if he never recognizes himself.' It was a mysterious answer that no one could decipher. As a youth, Narcissus was so beautiful that many people, both men and women, fell in love with him, but he rejected them all. One of his spurned admirers prayed to Nemesis, who damned Narcissus to pine away with love for his own beautiful face, as it was reflected in the waters of a pond on Mount Helicon. The longer he gazed at his own image, the more deeply he became infatuated with himself. This passionate self-love refused to wane; day after day he lay beside the pond, until he finally wasted away and died."[26]

The following legend from India combines the story of Narcissus with an account of the loneliness suffered by the first humans. After its protagonist wandered the world alone, "he saw himself in the mirror-like surface of a body of water and cried out, 'This is the most beautiful creature of all.' He ceaselessly searched the entire world to find that beautiful phantom, not knowing that he was actually hunting for himself....When the Creator saw this, He said to Himself, 'Alas, this is a difficulty I did not predict....I must find some remedy for this ailment....Some third entity is needed'....So he gathered up the reflections from the surface of the water and made a woman from them."[27] Since these reflections are those of the first man, the woman in this tale is also created—at least indirectly—from that man. Thus, this legend offers further evidence of the correctness of the dual-souls doctrine.

In his version of the Faust legend, Goethe also describes the vision of a lover in a mirror. Verse 3332ff suggests that this apparition involves a twin soul, especially when Goethe has Faust declare: "I am close to her and, no matter how far from her I might be, I would never forget her, never lose her."

We should note that, according to the dual-souls doctrine, a bond exists between the two soul companions that can never be torn asunder, regardless of how far apart they may have temporarily been separated.

Therefore shall a man leave his father and his mother, and shall cleave unto his wife: and they shall be one flesh.
(2:24)

The phrase that states that the man shall cling to his wife is particularly significant. This man is not simply seeking a suitable spouse or some other woman, but is binding himself to his wife, and it is clear that the Bible intends this wife to be none other than his dual soul. The statement that man and wife "shall be one flesh" refers to the physical union between the two; it also indicates the communal life they share in marriage. The original meaning of the phrases "sexual intercourse" and "bond of matrimony" was to signify that husband and wife belong to one another utterly and completely. Accordingly, wedding and sexual intercourse were intended to take place only between the two members of this dyad of souls. Of course, this variety of profound love for one another has unfortunately become the exception rather than the rule in our present day and age, but that is another story.

Rudolf Passian quotes Elisabeth Schramm-Schober in this context: "Unfortunately this knowledge about soul mates has been completely forgotten by the general public. Consequently, people today dissipate and distract themselves in tawdry adventures and...experience the same old thing with each new sexual partner rather than experiencing all things anew with the same partner."[28]

Genesis 2:24 (cited above) prophesies that, at some future date, when soul mates have taken on mundane bodies through their gestation and birth from their mothers' wombs, they (not only the man) will both leave their parents and bind themselves to one another in the same way that their parents once united with each other, and as they (the soul mates) were united prior to the initial division of the primal hermaphrodite. This latter state of being, of course, refers to their condition as spiritual entities who, rather than being born of physical mothers, were created as unborn entities emanated from the divine substance. It would be a mistake to interpret the words "father" and "mother" as referring to the divine substance that the man must abandon when he unites with his wife. Such an abandonment would mean turning away from God, thus making the marital union sinful. If it were sinful, it would no doubt have been incorporated into the description of the fall from grace, as told in Genesis 3.

Paul refers to Genesis 2:24 in his epistle to the Ephesians (see Ephesians 5:31): "Husbands, love your wives, even as Christ also loved the Church" (Ephesians 5:25) and "For no man ever yet hated his own flesh, but nourisheth and cherisheth it, even as the Lord the Church." (Ephesians 5:29) Moreover, "So ought men to love their wives as their own bodies. He that loveth his wife loveth himself" (Ephesians 5:28) reveals obvious parallels with the mirror stories described in our commentary on Genesis 2:23.

The Koran likewise contains a number of passages that point to the intimate link between husband and wife and provide guidelines for their proper dealings with one another: "He it is who hath created you from a single person, and from him brought forth his wife that he might dwell with her." (Sura 7:190) "And one of His signs it is that He hath created wives for you of your own species, that ye may dwell with them, and hath put love and tenderness between you. Herein truly are signs for those who reflect." (Sura 30:22)

48

The true and profound meaning of Genesis 2:24 is eloquently expressed in Plato's *Symposium*. After the original hermaphroditic human was cut in half by Zeus as a punishment for its undue audacity, "each—desiring its own half—came together and, throwing their arms around one another and entangling themselves with one another in their desire to grow together, they began to die off due to hunger and inactivity, because they were unwilling to do anything apart from one another....But Zeus took pity on them and supplied another means. He rearranged their genitals toward the front—for up until then they had them on the backside [No doubt this is an allegorical description of the original back-to-back connection between the male and female halves of the primal hermaphrodite], and they generated and gave birth not in one another but on the earth, like cicadas. And, for this purpose, he changed this part of them toward the front, and by this means made generation possible in one another...so that, in embracing, if a man meets a woman, they might generate and the race continue. [This statement can be seen as parallel to Genesis 3:16, in which, after the fall from grace, God speaks to Eve, saying: "I will greatly multiply thy sorrow and thy conception; in sorrow thou shalt bring forth children."] So it has been from early times that human beings have had, inborn in themselves, Eros for one another—Eros, the original unifier of their primordial nature, who tries to make one out of two and to heal human nature. When a guest leaves us, it is our custom to divide a token with him, and each keep half, and later we can recognize one another by looking at the two halves. Each of us, then, is a token of a human being, because we are sliced like fillets of sole, two out of one; and so each is always in search of his own token."

Aristophanes summarizes his view in the following closing remarks: "This was our ancient nature and we were whole. Love is the name for the desire and pursuit of the whole. And previously, as I say, we were one; but now through our injustice we have been dispersed by God." We will discuss the deeper meaning of Eros (i.e., sexual intercourse) in greater detail in Chapters Five and Seven.

As far as the change in the manner of procreation is concerned, Helena P. Blavatsky says, "this did not occur suddenly, as some people might assume, but required a long period of time before it became the sole 'natural' way."[29] According to the Vayu Purana that Blavatsky cites, "birth first proceeded from an egg, then from mist, then from vegetation, then from the pores of the skin and then, finally, from the womb."[30] Blavatsky concludes "every living creature and everything on Earth, including humankind, evolved from a common basic form. The physical human being must have progressed through the same stages of evolution and various types of procreation as did the other animals. He must have divided himself; then, as a hermaphrodite, brought forth his children through parthenogenesis [according to the principle of immaculate conception]. The next stage was the oviparous phase, at first *without any fertilizing element*, and then later *with help of the fertilizing spore*. Only after the final evolution could the two genders—male and female—come into being, as procreation through sexual union gradually became a universal law."[31]

Hermann Rudolph speaks to this theme: "It is said that there was a time on Earth when human beings were not divided into men and women and, as a consequence of the ethereal structure of their bodies, possessed the ability to procreate themselves inwardly by engendering a new form themselves, a form in which they continued their lives....Humanity's decline into physical conception is equivalent to humanity's fall from grace."[32]

Now that our examination of this change in the type of procreation and its various possibilities has led us somewhat afield

from the actual meaning contained in the words of Genesis 2:24, it behooves us to turn our attention to Swedenborg, who describes the deeper meaning of marriage: "Marriage is the form in which man and woman not only merge, but also become *one flesh*, which we can best translate in the words *a new creature* or *a new person*."[33] I will refrain from any further commentary here about Genesis 2:24, since I will discuss this verse in greater depth in Chapters Five and Seven.

And they were both naked, the man and his wife, and they were not ashamed. (2:25)

At first, soul mates recognized that they belonged together but, while they seemed to be of opposite genders, at this point in time (i.e., before the fall from grace described in the third chapter of Genesis) they were not yet subject to mundane passions. Because they were still pure spirits and still dwelt in ethereal bodies, they were unaware of their nakedness and, thus, also of the difference between their genders. The Persian myth of Meschia (the primal male human) and Meschiane (the primal female human) confirms what I wrote above, since both were intimately linked to one another and completely identical in appearance. In the creation stories of the Kaiva Kamu clan recounted in Chapter One, the first human couple was likewise neither male nor female since they were not furnished with sexual organs. Only later did Kerema Apo become a man and Ivi Apo become a woman.

Verse 2:25 indicates that soul mates initially dwelt in a state of perfect oneness and had not lost their innocence. Despite their nakedness, they were unashamed. Only after the fall from grace did they become aware of their nakedness and feel shame. This probably means that, at that point in time, they did not yet know about sexual intercourse. Their affection for one another took the form of spiritual intercourse, a blossoming of one soul within the other. This type of intimate union can be understood as a celestial precursor to the earthly variety of sexual intercourse that arose later. It was entirely free of base lusts and was characterized by the purest love and most complete surrender to one another. This explains why they had no reason to feel shame. Before the fall from grace, they had no notion of "cheating" on one another (i.e., of entering into intimate union with one half of any other dyad).

Edgar Cayce agrees with this view: "The separation of the genders had already begun. However, this could not be described as a sin since, when the divine androgynous entities split into pairs of companions (e.g., Amilius and Lilith), they preserved their original purity and did not lust after the fleshy forms of the Earth."[34]

We find further evidence for the truth of this thesis among the Wa, a group of people who live in the region between Indonesia and China. According to the Wa creation myth, the original beings, Yatawm and Yatai, "were neither spirits nor humans. Although they seemed to be of different genders, they felt no mundane passions." Only later, after they ate two gourds that the Creator had caused to fall onto the Earth near them, and after they sowed the seeds of those gourds, which sprouted and became new gourds and ultimately grew into a whole hill of gourds, only then did they become aware of sexual passion."[35] This creation myth reminds us of Eve's and Adam's partaking of the forbidden fruit and their subsequent recognition of their own nakedness, as described in Genesis 3:6-7.

52

3. THE FALL FROM GRACE

The fall from grace—also known as "original sin"—described in the third chapter of Genesis has raised countless questions and led to an enormous range of interpretations and speculations. Every conceivable explanation has been explored. Some interpreters vilify the snake, citing the temptation of humankind by the devil in the form of a serpent and the subsequent exile into a sinful world. Other exegetes claim that the snake actually helped humankind through its role as a tempter, by showing us the path to wisdom.

Genesis' account of the fall from grace evokes the impression of several so-called "original sins" and implies that the deeper meaning of these sins is hidden beneath the words of the biblical story, while at the same time forming the unifying foundation of the narrative. On the one hand, these sins involve transgression against the highest God (i.e., against the primal principle and the unity of life). On the other hand, the fall from grace involves a thoroughly justified, and perhaps even necessary, transgression against the single-handedly established commandments and prohibitions established by the Elohim, the authors and rulers of the visible, material world.

The following quotations help explain the reasons for my belief that the story of the fall from grace is in fact a concatenation of several different tales.

Genesis 3:4,5,22 and 24 support the second interpretation; namely, that the serpent is a benefactor of humanity, and that those who make the laws are not identical with the highest God (i.e., the God of love and the source of all life), but rather are gods of lower rank who have fallen away from the primal principle through their own wrongdoing. In Genesis 3:4 and 5, the serpent explains to Eve: "in the day ye eat thereof, then your eyes shall be opened, and ye shall be as gods, knowing good and evil."

The Koran contains a similar account of the temptation. According to the Islamic version, Satan promises eternal life: "This tree hath your Lord forbidden you, only lest ye should become angels, or lest ye should become immortals." (Sura 7:21)

It is obvious that neither the snake in Genesis nor Satan in the Koran were lying. This leads to a serious question: Why should acquiring the knowledge of good and evil be described as a sinful act? No less an authoritative voice than that of God Himself confirms the depth and truth of this newly acquired knowledge when He says, "Behold, the man has become as one of us, to know good and evil." (3:22) It is not easy to find the deeper meaning behind these words. After God said, "Let us make man in our image, after our likeness," (1:26) and after the Bible specifically states that "God created man in His own image, in the image of God," (1:27) why is it that now the even greater similarity between God and man, represented by man's acquisition of the knowledge of good and evil, is suddenly judged to be sinful? An alternate interpretation is possible, however, that confirms the first-mentioned explanation; namely that, in the beginning, man was necessarily good simply because he had no notion of evil. Only after acquiring knowledge of good and evil, did it become possible for him to differentiate between these two poles. Although the soul as such is fundamentally good, and although it strives for goodness, it has a tendency toward negative thoughts and actions that obscure its view of true goodness and make union with that goodness nearly impossible.

According to Genesis 3:22, the Lord continued: "And now, lest he put forth his hand and take also of the tree of life, and eat and live for ever!" This second phrase and the subsequent place-ment of cherubim armed with a flaming sword (3:24) to bar the way to the tree of life suggest that the speaker of this passage is not the highest God, who is a God of love and the origin of us all. Instead, it seems that these verses must have been spoken by lesser gods who had themselves fallen away from God and at-tained power over the material cosmos but not over the spiritual world of the upper regions. It seems likely that the frequently mentioned "evil gods" are identical with the "lords of the shadow world," the gnostic demiurge (builder of the world) and the Chris-tian devil, all of who want to keep souls imprisoned in the cycle of birth and rebirth. These "evil gods" do everything in their power to prevent humankind from acquiring genuine knowledge of God so that, in its ignorance, humanity will be unable to enter the upper realms and achieve immortality. It only makes sense to talk about "immortality" when there can be no more death. That, in fact, is the goal of every religion—namely, to overcome death and attain eternal life. Paradoxically, the speakers in these biblical verses regard achievement of this goal as a negative development for humanity that must be prevented at all costs.

Further support for this interpretation can be derived from the fact that there exists only one *highest God*. But the God who speaks in this passage says, "Let *us* make man in our image, after *our* likeness" (Genesis 1:26) and afterward declares "Be-hold, the man is become as one of *us*." (3:22) This voice appears to be expressing the feelings of a group, and thus could not be that of the one and only highest God.

John A. Phillips agrees with this conclusion: "Earlier readers of the holy scripture were fully aware that these events in the garden of Eden might just as well have been described as a bless-ing rather than a curse. Maimonides (1135-1204) mentions what would seem to be a long-standing objection to Jewish dogma—namely, the absurdity that the consequences of man's disobedi-ence are none other than 'reason, the ability to think and the capacity to differentiate between good and evil.' Centuries earlier, the gnostic authors held the view that knowledge per se must necessarily be good. Since the creator god is not identical with the one true God, but is a subordinate being, Adam's and Eve's uprising against Yahweh would be a virtue and the snake would be a benefactor of humankind, a teacher who brings us the fundamental knowledge of good and evil that the creator attempted to keep hidden from us."[1]

Helena P. Blavatsky provides us with a corresponding report. According to her, Ilda Baoth (whom various sects looked upon as the god of Moses) was not a pure spirit, but created a world of his own and rejected the spiritual light of his mother Sophia Achamoth. "Eager to separate man from his spiritual guardian, Ilda Baoth forbade Adam and Eve to eat of his fruit. Sophia Achamoth, who loved and protected the man whom she had brought to life, sent her own genius (Orphis) in the form of a snake to persuade Eve and Adam to overstep this selfish and unrighteous command."[2] Helena P. Blavatsky further claims that the snake is identical with Adam Kadmon—man and wife—who become Orphis and try to taste the fruits of the tree of good and evil and, thus, learn the mysteries of spiritual wisdom.[3]

The alert reader might find this to be a contradiction. On the one hand, it is said that the Elohim (the beings who had fallen away from God) established the world. On the other hand, it is said that the material universe was created so that those beings who had fallen away from God (and who later incarnated as humans, animals, or other forms) would have something to which they could cling. These two apparently contradictory hypotheses can be reconciled when we realize that the Elohim were still pure in spirit and in harmony with the primal principle when they acted *on behalf* of that primal power and established the visible cosmos as a foothold for fallen souls. Later on, however, the Elohim became so infatuated with their own creation that they dedicated themselves to that world (of their own creation), thus turning their faces away from the primal principle. Because the material world gave them such immense pleasure, they wanted to preserve it and, as much as possible, keep incarnated beings imprisoned within it. For this reason, they commanded those beings to "be fruitful, and multiply and replenish the earth." (Genesis 1:28)

Verses 3:7, 3:14 and 3:21 appear to disagree with this version of the fall from grace and support instead the interpretation we presented first. Verse 7, for example, tells us that, just as the serpent had promised, "the eyes of them both were opened" and because their eyes were now open, "they knew that they were naked" and "sewed fig leaves together and made themselves aprons" to hide their nakedness. According to Athanasius the Great's insightful interpretation, they did not recognize their nakedness in a physical sense, but realized that they were naked in their beholding of divine things and that their thoughts had been directed toward worldly things.

Sura 7:23 of the Koran corresponds with the account in Genesis 3:7. The Koran says: "So he beguiled them by deceits. When they had tasted of the tree, their nakedness appeared to them and they began to sew together upon themselves the leaves of the garden."

Hebrew mythology tells that first Chavah (Eve) lost her radiant outer skin, a raiment of light as fine as a fingernail, and afterward Adam sinned as well. But, before he fell from grace, Adam "wrestled three hours against the temptation to eat and become like her. During the hours of this struggle he held the fruit in his hand. Finally he said, 'Chavah, I would rather die than outlive you. If death should claim your soul, God could never console me with any other woman, even if her beauty were as great as yours!' With these words, Adam ate the fruit and his raiment of light fell from him, too."[4]

An ancient Persian myth may well be a source of the story of the fall from grace as recounted in Genesis. According to the Persian account: "Meschia and Meschiane originally ate only fruits [i.e., in obedience to God's commandment (see Genesis 1:29)], but were later seduced by the demon Ahriman, who persuaded them to disobey God. They lost their purity, cut down trees, killed animals and committed other misdeeds."[5]

Leo Schaya's view of the fall from grace and its consequences agrees with kabbalistic teachings. According to Schaya: "Because they [the sinful entities] clung to the pleasure of their existence, they forgot to affirm God, who is the source and meaning of their lives. Their self-affirmation finally degenerated into the negation of their own eternal, primal essence, which is God, and His divine grace assumed an element of severity in order to negate this negation. Out of *Chesed* came forth *Din* (judgment). Din is the severe judgment upon all things that sets boundaries to the affirmation of all creatures; the outermost boundary thereof is death and hell."[6]

Genesis further reports that Adam and Eve "hid themselves from the presence of the Lord God" (3:8) and that "the Lord God called unto Adam, and said unto him, 'Where art thou?'" (3:9) "And he said, 'I heard thy voice in the garden and I was afraid because I was naked and I hid myself.'" (3:10) "And He said, 'Who told thee that thou wast naked? Hast thou eaten of the tree whereof I commanded thee that thou shouldest not eat?'" (3:11) "And Adam said, 'The woman whom Thou gavest to be with me, she gave me of the tree, and I did eat.'" (3:12) "And the Lord God said unto the woman, 'What is this that thou has done?' And the woman said, 'The serpent beguiled me, and I did eat.'" (3:13) "And the Lord God said unto the serpent, 'Because thou hast done this, thou art cursed above all cattle and above every beast of the field; upon thy belly shalt thou go, and dust shalt thou eat all the days of thy life.'" (3:14)

The serpent symbolizes man's fall and the consequences for which he is held responsible. Because of the phalloid shape of its body, the snake symbolizes sexuality; because it sheds its skin, it also symbolizes reincarnation (birth, death and rebirth) through various bodies. God condemns the serpent to creep upon

the earth and eat dust. This means that fallen man must continually be born into new bodies on Earth or on other planets, at
least until he is redeemed. Thus, he remains confined within the
cycle of becoming (*samsara*). It also means that man is obliged
to eat mundane foods to nourish his body and keep it alive. As a
giant serpent, Oceanos twines himself around the entire created
world. Ourobouros, the mighty snake that bites its own tail, is a
symbol for the endless cycle of coming into being and passing
out of existence.

As we will see in subsequent passages, because of its own (temporary) base instincts, the soul is obliged to incarnate in body after
body. As a result of its own desires and needs, but not as a divine
punishment, the soul remains imprisoned within the physical realm
(the cycle of coming into being and passing out of existence.)

In the next passage (Genesis 3:15), the Lord God says to the
serpent: "I will put enmity between thee and the woman, and
between thy seed and her seed." Since the snake symbolizes
another fallen creature, this verse is ultimately trying to tell us
that humankind has fallen away from harmonious cosmic unity
and descended into a world where everyone fights with everyone else. Further support for the view that this represents a fallen
state is found in the allegorical story of Cain and Abel.

Verse 3:21 continues the tale: "Unto Adam also and to his wife
did the Lord God make coats of skins, and clothed them."
Origenes correctly realizes that these coats of skins refer to the
human body itself, which was originally covered with a much
thicker pelt of hair than it has today. Origenes asks the rhetorical
question, "Is God a tanner or a maker of saddles, that He should
sew coats of skin for Adam and Eve?" He rejects this assumption as patently absurd and concludes, "It is therefore obvious
that Moses is referring to our own bodies."

The gnostic philosophy espoused by the Ophites takes a similar view of this passage: "In the past, and in accord with their

creation [in heaven], the bodies of Adam and Eve were light, luminous and spiritual; when they fell from grace, their bodies became darker, denser and more sluggish." Clad in these heavier bodies, they "were obliged to contemplate themselves and realize that, on their own, they were naked and mortal and bore death within them. Thus, they learned to patiently accept the realization that, at least for a certain length of time, they must remain clothed and enclosed within this mundane body."[7]

At the beginning of this chapter it seemed useful to examine more closely the two fundamentally different interpretations of the fall from grace and to call particular attention to those verses that would support one or the other of these interpretations. In this context, we are primarily interested in the first of these interpretations because we want to place most emphasis on the first fall, also known as "original sin." This event marks a falling away from the unity of all life, the loss of a paradisiacal state in which there is neither death nor transience. It initiates the decline into a state of existence characterized by coming into being and ceasing to be, by the painful experience of repeated births and deaths. The fall from grace is also known as the "spiritual fall," and one of its consequences is the establishment of the material cosmos. Since the essential nature of the soul is bodiless, there can be no doubt that souls must have committed some sort of transgression that led to their incarnation into bodies. Of course, I could just as well have placed this discussion about the fall from grace at the outset of this book. I ultimately decided to place it here, however, so that the sequence of my own first three chapters would more closely parallel the sequence of events described in Genesis. As we have seen, the biblical account begins with a description of the creation of the androgynous human, follows by recounting the division of that entity and only then deals with the fall from grace.

Of course, we are especially interested in those events surrounding the fall from grace that clearly confirm the story of the divi-

sion of the originally androgynous human into two genders, a
division we have already discussed at length in the preceding
chapter. At the beginning of Genesis 3, the snake asks Eve
whether God has forbidden her and Adam from eating from all
the trees in the garden. Eve answers that she and Adam are per-
mitted to "eat of the fruit of the trees of the garden. But the fruit
of the tree that is in the midst of the garden, God hath said, 'Ye
shall not eat of it.'" (Genesis 3:2-3) Comparing Genesis 2:16
and 2:17 we see that, as mentioned in the preceding chapter,
God commanded *the man* not to eat of that tree, yet in Genesis
3:3 it is *the woman* who cites the receipt of this commandment.
Eve's recitation of God's commandment is another piece of evidence in support of my assertion that man and woman must originally have formed a single entity and were later divided. If, at
the time the commandment was spoken, she had not yet been
crafted out of the rib of a preexisting man, she would surely not
have responded to the snake by citing the divine prohibition. At
the moment when God spoke the commandment recounted in
Genesis 2:16-17, the woman had not yet been given to the man
and, according to exoteric interpretations, she did not even exist. Not until Genesis 2:22 was she formed and brought to the
man. How, then, could she possibly have known about God's
commandment? In chapters 2:16-17, God speaks to the man as
follows: "Of every tree of the garden thou mayest freely eat. But
of the tree of the knowledge of good and evil, thou shalt not eat
of it, for in the day that thou eatest thereof thou shalt surely die."
It is to this commandment that the woman alludes in her re-
sponse to the snake in Genesis 3:3.

All in all, disobedience to the commandment of the highest
God—and, thus, also the turning away from Him and toward
other things, the desire for which can only be fulfilled in the
material realm—ought to be regarded as the central point of the
original fall from grace. This satisfaction of needs that can only
be fulfilled in the material realm not only led to the embodiment of the soul within a material body, but also caused its
bondage within the cycle of death and rebirth. Only after the

soul has rid itself of this sort of desire can it free itself from the cycle.

This means that the soul must overcome desires that can only be fulfilled in the material realm. It can achieve this liberation only through inner realization and conviction. We would, however, be completely mistaken if we were to try to suppress these desires, since that would only result in the opposite of liberation. When a previously contented soul, who has been trying to satisfy its desires, attempts instead to suppress those desires (which nonetheless continue to exist because they have not yet been overcome through inner conviction), that soul is sure to suffer self-imposed torture. This is neither intended nor in any way beneficial.

We can assume that *in the beginning* (i.e., at a "time" prior to time and "before" the creation of the material universe) souls (i.e., sparks from the divine Spirit) lived together in a harmonious community. At some point, a change must have occurred within this community, causing some souls to strive against the primal principle (which we generally call "God"). At first there were probably only a few renegade souls—who, considered together, symbolize the "devil," the first entity to fall away from God. Later more and more souls followed this bad example, lured by the possibilities that the fallen souls promised them if they would turn away from the community and toward their own individuality. This state of affairs is allegorically represented as seduction by the devil, or snake. Succumbing to the lure of individuality, these souls also fell away from the unity of the primal principle, becoming distinct and isolated individuals—much as drops of water separate from the wholeness of the watery element and become a myriad of individual droplets.

This view is corroborated by a statement in Herbert Engel's *Sphärenwanderer*, in which it is written that we all once lived and acted from the power of the spirit.[8] This text also states that this *action* originally took place in harmony with the will of the primal power.[9] "But someone must have started it—at first a few of us, then more of us, began to have peculiar thoughts. We wanted to know just how great was the extent of our freedom to independently determine our own actions."[10] On the next page of this book, Engel tells us that only one portion of the entities fell away from unity. These fallen souls later received help from those who had not fallen.[11]

Origenes holds a similar view. According to him, "Souls were motivated to take on bodies either because of desire or because of a sense of duty." Those who were motivated by desire succumbed to the temptation to indulge their sensual lusts. Those who were motivated by a sense of duty felt the need to serve God, and to help other souls who had become embodied due to desire, to remind them of their divine origins and to lead them back to God. Despite the nobility of their motives, only a few of these "pure servants" were able to remain free of sensual lusts. Many of them, although originally incarnated out of a sense of duty to God or their fellow creatures, succumbed to the temptation of sensuality. Thus, they suffered the same fate as those whom they had incarnated to redeem. Regardless of whether they fell away from God earlier or later, all these souls are subject to the repeated pains of many births and deaths. And all of them share the same mission— namely, to liberate themselves from their physical fetters so they can return to God in the realm of light. In agreement with the thesis set forth above, Origenes further teaches that "all bodiless and invisible yet reasonable creatures, when they fall into negligence, gradually slide downward to lower stages. They take on various bodies, depending on the characteristics of the place to which they have sunk (e.g., first bodies of ether, then of air). When they approach the Earth, they surround themselves with even denser bodies, until they are finally fettered to human flesh." (*de princ*. I,5) According to Origenes, this change in the character of souls is accompanied by a change in their status.

All the entities who originally emanated from God owe their existence to the *one life*; all of them are, and have always been, fragments of the *one life*. Although they are discrete, individual entities, they have not misunderstood their individuality. They continue to dwell in the community and for the community. They can be compared to drops of water that, considered together, compose *one ocean*, yet continue to exist separately as a true community within that ocean. The frequently misunderstood "parable of water" that Eastern scriptures propose as an explanation of life clearly does not entail the annihilation of the individual in nirvana, but only means that each individual is part of a oneness that ultimately leads to its union with all others. Each individual drop of water undergoes the same process: although they all merge to become an ocean, this does not imply that each drop passes out of existence. Perhaps each one unites with an infinite number of other droplets and, thus, becomes one with them all.

Consciousness of individuality is an essential element of the first fall from grace. This does not entail becoming conscious of an *ego,* as such, but rather derives from the arrogant illusion that the individual is a fully independent entity and is therefore no longer bound to God.

I would like to introduce another parable here that, I hope, will make it clear that the *one life*, which is identical with the *God of love*, has a vested interest in retrieving each and every *lost entity* (i.e., creatures like us, who have become lost in the midst of our cosmic peregrinations). God wants to lead all of us "lost sheep" home to our original oneness. To understand this parable, we can imagine the substance of life as a jigsaw puzzle. I freely admit that this parable is not perfect, simply because, although God dwells within all beings, He does not undergo any changes. But, despite the imperfections of the puzzle parable, it is still useful. On the one hand, the individual being, like a single piece in a gigantic puzzle, is nothing on his or her own and knows nothing of the whole picture. On the other hand, each piece in the puzzle (i.e., each individual) is important and irreplaceable since the puzzle cannot be solved to yield a complete picture if even one piece is missing.

Since all life originally arose from the One Being and "without Him was not any thing made that was made," (John 1:3) it is clear that even the devil (or Satan in the Koran, who led Adam and Eve to their fall; or the serpent in the Bible, who was responsible for that same seduction) must trace his origins to this same supreme Oneness. However, the devil must have already fallen away from that unity prior to the fall from grace described in the Bible and the Koran.

Origenes teaches likewise: "If, as some people believe, the nature of the devil were darkness, how could he once have been the morning star? And if there were nothing luminous in him, how could he rise and shine in the early morning? Our Savior teaches us about the nature of the devil when He says (in Luke 10:18) 'I beheld Satan as lightning falling from heaven.' This shows that the devil was once light." (*de princ.* I:5)

The narrative of the expulsion from paradise (or the falling away of a certain number of souls from the primal unity of all life) is recounted in verses 3:23 and 24 of Genesis. "Therefore the Lord God sent him forth from the garden of Eden, to till the ground from whence he was taken. So he drove out the man, and he placed cherubim to the east of the garden of Eden, and a flaming sword that turned in every direction, to keep the way of the tree of life." (Genesis 3:23-24)

To conclude this chapter, we should again recall something I already mentioned at the beginning of the chapter—namely, that Genesis' account of the fall from grace involves more than one original sin. Some of these sins were against the highest God (and, thus, against ourselves), others were cases of disobedience to the Elohim (the builders of the material world). These acts of disobedience were necessary in order to escape from the Elohim and, ultimately, to reunite with the God of love, who is the ultimate substance of life itself.

Paradise, the garden of Eden, as described in the Bible, never existed anywhere on Earth, but is located in the astral region. The Koran corroborates this assertion in Sura 7 in which God says, "Get ye down [onto the Earth], the one of you an enemy to the other, and earth shall be your dwelling, and your provision for a season." (7:25) The enmity that rages between earthly creatures becomes all too obvious when strife breaks out between Cain and Abel. The verse continues, "He said, 'On it shall ye live, and on it shall ye die, and from it shall ye be taken forth.'" (7:26) able since the puzzle cannot be solved to yield a complete picture if even one piece is missing.

Since all life originally arose from the One Being and "without Him was not any thing made that was made," (John 1:3) it is clear that even the devil (or Satan in the Koran, who led Adam and Eve to their fall; or the serpent in the Bible, who was responsible for that same seduction) must trace his origins to this same supreme Oneness. However, the devil must have already fallen away from that unity prior to the fall from grace described in the Bible and the Koran.

Origenes teaches likewise: "If, as some people believe, the nature of the devil were darkness, how could he once have been the morning star? And if there were nothing luminous in him, how could he rise and shine in the early morning? Our Savior teaches us about the nature of the devil when He says (in Luke 10:18) 'I beheld Satan as lightning falling from heaven.' This shows that the devil was once light." (*de princ.* I:5)

The narrative of the expulsion from paradise (or the falling away of a certain number of souls from the primal unity of all life) is recounted in verses 3:23 and 24 of Genesis. "Therefore the Lord God sent him forth from the garden of Eden, to till the ground from whence he was taken. So he drove out the man, and he placed cherubim to the east of the garden of Eden, and a flaming sword that turned in every direction, to keep the way of the tree of life." (Genesis 3:23-24)

To conclude this chapter, we should again recall something I already mentioned at the beginning of the chapter—namely, that Genesis' account of the fall from grace involves more than one original sin. Some of these sins were against the highest God (and, thus, against ourselves), others were cases of disobedience to the Elohim (the builders of the material world). These acts of disobedience were necessary in order to escape from the Elohim and, ultimately, to reunite with the God of love, who is the ultimate substance of life itself.

Paradise, the garden of Eden, as described in the Bible, never existed anywhere on Earth, but is located in the astral region. The Koran corroborates this assertion in Sura 7 in which God says, "Get ye down [onto the Earth], the one of you an enemy to the other, and earth shall be your dwelling, and your provision for a season." (7:25) The enmity that rages between earthly creatures becomes all too obvious when strife breaks out between Cain and Abel. The verse continues, "He said, 'On it shall ye live, and on it shall ye die, and from it shall ye be taken forth.'" (7:26)

*And Adam knew Eve his wife, and she conceived, and bare
Cain, and said, 'I have gotten a man from the Lord'.
(Genesis 4:1)*

Some interval of time must have passed between this fourth chapter and the expulsion from paradise recounted in Genesis 3:23-
24. According to this version, Adam and Eve were not yet adults
immediately after their expulsion, but would first have been born
on Earth, most likely by taking on material bodies directly out
of the soil. They would not have suddenly appeared on Earth as
full-grown adults, but would have had to pass through all the
stages of ordinary growth. They would have been born as in-
fants, then gradually grown through the years of childhood and
puberty, and finally met one another. This seems to be the meaning of the biblical words "and Adam knew Eve his wife." If,
after their expulsion from the celestial paradise, they had retained their sinful consciousness (i.e., if, when they arrived on
Earth, they had still remembered their sacrilege), and if they had
immediately incarnated as full-grown adults on Earth, it would
not have been necessary for Adam to know—or to *recognize*—
his wife, since she would have been beside him the whole time.
They must, therefore, have been born as children in some way
(perhaps directly out of the earth) and spent their childhoods in
separate places until they were old enough and the predetermined
time had come for them to encounter one another again. Adam
recognized Eve and they stayed together. Eve expresses her joy
at having found her true mate and not being obliged to settle for

some other spouse with the words, "I have gotten a man *from* [i.e., with the help of] *the Lord.*"

According to Edgar Cayce, despite their plunge into the material realm, "human beings still remained relatively close to God and, during their first millennium on Earth, were incarnated in bodies that enabled their souls to express themselves with much greater ease than would be the case later on. Occult abilities were everyday occurrences....But human beings moved further and further away from their origin, submerged themselves ever more deeply in the material world with all its mundane attractions and gradually lost their God-given powers."[1]

As early as their first incarnation, human beings had already begun to identify themselves more with the Earth than with their previous and true home. The fact that they immediately bore children (Eve became pregnant and bore Cain) is evidence of this shift in identification. Thus, they gradually strayed further and further into the cycle of repeated births and deaths.

And Cain knew his wife. (4:17)

After reading this biblical verse (if not before), anyone who interprets the myths about the division of the original human pair to mean that the separation of genders was a one-time-only process involving only the original couple (i.e., Adam and Eve, according to biblical tradition) so they could conceive descendants, should earnestly consider revising his or her preconceived opinions. Furthermore, anyone who believes that, because these descendants were conceived by human parents and not split into two genders, they could not have possessed soul mates, must question the validity of his or her beliefs (or the beliefs in which he or she was indoctrinated by the Christian church). People who favor this interpretation are likely to be among those who deny the previous existence of the soul and who, instead, persist in adhering to the erroneous notion that the eternal soul is conceived together with the transitory body and that the soul, although it came into being simultaneously with the body, outlives the body and abandons that body after its death.

Origenes, the best-known ancient Christian scholar, speaks to this theme: "How could the soul of him, of whom God said, 'Before I formed thee in the belly, I knew thee; and before thou camest forth out of the womb I sanctified thee' (Jeremiah 1:5) have been formed together with his body? It cannot be that God would imbue individuals with the Holy Spirit at random, rather than selecting those individuals according to their maturity; nor could it be that God would sanctify people without their having earned sanctification. How else could we explain the meaning of the words, 'Is there unrighteousness with God? God forbid' (Romans 9:14) What else could 'For there is no respect of persons with God' (Romans 2:11) possibly mean? These contradictions would be the consequences of a doctrine asserting that the soul came into being together with the body." (*de princ.* I7:4)

First of all, we must clearly understand that "at no time whatsoever is the soul born nor does it die. Neither is the soul a thing that comes into being only once and, after it passes away, will never again come into being. The soul is unborn, primordial and everlasting. It cannot be slain when the body is slain." (Bhagavad Gita 2:20) This is because "there never was a time when I, you and these kings did not exist. Nor shall there ever come a future time when any one of us shall no longer exist." (Bhagavad Gita 2:12) In Plato's *Republic*, Socrates explains the eternal nature of the soul in words whose clarity must be self-evident to every rational person: "Then, if there is no evil that can destroy it [the soul], either its own or another's [evil], it must exist forever; that is to say, it must be immortal....We can take that, then, as proven....And, if so, it follows that the same souls have always existed. Their number cannot be decreased because no soul can die, nor can it increase. Any increase in the immortal must be at the expense of mortality and, if that were possible, everything would in the end be immortal."[2]

The Indian philosopher Radhakrishnan explains: "The herd, the endless host of souls, belongs to the Lord. He is not their Creator since they are eternal. The soul is different from the body, which is an unconscious object of experience....For the duration of her temporal existence, the soul unites with the thing in which she dwells....The number of souls neither increases nor decreases. As the number of souls who find redemption increases, the number of unredeemed souls decreases correspondingly. Consciousness is fully manifest in the redeemed souls, but in the embodied ones it is obscured."[3]

Since all souls come into being everlastingly and from the same primal substance, they must also all share the same essence. If all souls begin with the same essence, all of them (i.e., all the souls currently incarnated in physical bodies) must have undergone the same process of division into two genders. In other words, if Adam and Eve individuated from one entity, and are thus soul mates, this same situation must apply to all other entities as well. Consequently, for every soul who exists in a body of the one gender, there must also exist another soul incarnated in a body of the opposite gender. The aforementioned biblical verse supports this conclusion: like his father before him, Cain, the son of Adam and Eve, also "knew his wife" (i.e., recognized the dual soul who belonged to him since the beginning of time). What other interpretation could this biblical verse possibly have?

And Adam knew his wife again. (4:25)

Since every human being knows the people with whom he has been connected in a particular manner for a long period of time, Adam really did not need to get to know Eve all over again. This biblical verse could refer to a subsequent incarnation (that would have taken place after the incarnation described in Genesis 4:1) since only in this context would Adam's "re-cognition" of Eve make logical sense.

Plato conveys the essential message of Genesis 4:25 in his *Symposium*, in which he places the following words about the recognition of two soul mates in Aristophanes' mouth. According to Aristophanes, when one "meets with that very one who is his own half, then they are wondrously struck with friendship, attachment and love, and are just about unwilling to be apart from one another even for a short time."

Rudolf Passian describes the case of a Viennese man named Herman Medinger who, after leaving his body as the result of an accident, believed that he encountered another being, who, in a kind of house of mirrors, told Medinger that he had often been together with him during his previous existences. In most of these past lives, the two of them had been happily united in marital embrace, although the gender roles each played had varied from incarnation to incarnation. During some past lives they had merely been close friends, while in others they had even been adversaries.[4]

Ronald Zürrer also writes about this theme: "Not only is it possible and probable that an intimate partnership should find its longed-for continuation in a subsequent existence, but it can also happen that both partners continue to exchange gender roles. Depending on whether our attachment to the other soul is stronger or weaker than our identification with our own gender-determined behavior, in our future lives we will either remain in our same gender roles or else return to Earth having traded genders with our partner. Each, clothed in a new body, once again bonds with his or her partner."[5]

Since, as we have already shown, souls are neither male nor female nor even human (in the sense of "human" referring to an ignorant, incarnated person), each soul takes on a new body according to that soul's karma. The Vedas ascribe to this view, asserting that the soul is neither male nor female, but transcends all the dualities of the material world. This explains why, in its next incarnation, a soul who is currently incarnated in a male body can enter a female body. It also explains why that same soul could just as well have animated and dwelt within a feminine body during its most recent past incarnation. Although this theme is quite interesting, we really have neither the time nor space to deal with it in greater depth here. Readers who are interested in this issue are urged to consult the relevant specialized literature.

As far as our theme is concerned, we need only note that the exchange of gender roles from one incarnation to the next by no means contradicts the dual-souls doctrine. Passian[6] and Dethlefsen agree. According to Dethlefsen, "After testing many hypotheses, our current opinion is that a soul possesses a fixed gender and that a corresponding dual soul of the opposite gender also exists. In the majority of its incarnations, a soul repeatedly enters into bodies having the same gender as the ones it entered at the beginning. Incarnations of the opposite gender are interspersed from time to time so that the soul can have particular experiences or redeem karma. The soul frequently (but not always) incarnates together with its dual soul, since the evolution of each is dependent upon the evolution of its counterpart."[7]

Peter Michel discusses the two fundamentally divergent opinions about the exchange of gender roles and the reasons for that interchange: "The source of the differences of opinion about the change of gender during the course of reincarnations lies in two different notions of the world. The one theory could be described as *evolutive*, the other as *creationist*."[8] According to the evolutive model, "the goal of evolution on the physical plane is to achieve a completely balanced human being composed partly of *masculine* attributes, such as volition and intelligence, and partly of *feminine* attributes, such as intuition and love; the fully evolved human being would manifest both aspects in complete perfection."[9]

Michel continues: "To achieve this goal, the soul changes its gender, thus accumulating experiences in both male and female bodies. The creationist model assumes that 'in the beginning' God created all beings as dyads. These dual-soul sparks wander together throughout creation, encounter one another again and again in the course of their evolutionary paths and ultimately live together in the complete and perfect harmony of divine consciousness. This model is surely the 'more poetic' one, and more than a few of the world's greatest poets have believed in it. When we behold the great mystery of love that has motivated human life in its most profound, essential core since time immemorial, it would seem that the attraction between opposite poles expresses a deeper wisdom than that found in the 'evolutive' model that reduces love, that eternal mystery, to a mere learning factor and an expeditious means of acquiring experience."[10]

Professor Ian Stevenson documents numerous cases of gender-role exchange in *Children Who Remember Previous Lives: A Question of Reincarnation* (Charlottesville: University Press of Virginia, 1987), a book that I recommend to readers interested in this theme. For example, Stevenson interviewed a Burmese girl named Tin Aung Myo, an American girl named Erin Jackson, an Indian girl named Rani Saxena and a Brazilian boy named Paulo Lorenz. All these children were able to recall previous existences in bodies of the opposite gender. Anyone who believes that the soul switches the gender of the body it enters in strict alternation, incarnating into a female body during one lifetime then into a male body during the next lifetime and so forth, will be compelled to abandon that belief after having read a few of the case studies published by Professor Stevenson.

An example of the gender switch and same-gender reincarnation of two closely linked entities is found in a case that Professor Stevenson studied. The Burmese twin girls Khin Ma Gyi and Hin Ma Nge were both able to recall the past lives of their maternal grandparents. Khin Ma Gyi recalled that she had been a man in her past life. As a small child, Khin Ma Gyi wore boy's clothes and displayed certain habits and traits that had been typical of her grandfather. Another example of gender reversal (undergone by newly incarnated souls) and renewed encounter in this lifetime is provided by the case of another pair of twin girls, Sivanthie and Sheromie Hettiaratchi, who were able to recall their past lives as two young men. These men had been close friends and homosexuals.

Both of these case studies involve couples who, either as husband and wife or as homosexual lovers, were close to one another in one or more past incarnations, perhaps throughout a very long period of time. In each case, they found one another again in the current incarnation, and could well be expected to find one another again in future lives. It seems, however, to be difficult for two lovers to be born together as twins, since these sibling soul mates cannot love one another in the same way as a pair of lovers of the opposite gender who are not related by blood.

Birth as twins is explained quite differently in the all too frequently misunderstood sense proposed by Christian theologians. Twin births occur when, having encountered one another in the astral realm (where souls dwell during the interval between incarnations), two souls do not wish to be separated from one another when the time comes for one of those souls to be reincarnated. (Scientists who have studied near-death phenomena report that when the soul leaves the body it is met by entities with whom it was intimately associated during the lifetime of the body from which it is now departing.) Since the two souls in the astral realm cannot bear to be separated, they enter the same womb at the same time and are subsequently born as twins. Both of the aforementioned case studies could well involve pairs of soul mates, but because this is not certain, there is no use speculating about it.

According to Indian tradition, one and the same goddess can appear at various times as the spouse, mother and sister of the same god. Although it might appear so at first glance, these various kinship arrangements need not necessarily contradict one another, but could suggest a more profound meaning. The following verses from an Upanishad (the name of which I do not know) describe just such a situation:

> *The breasts from which he drank before*
> *He later embraces lasciviously.*
> *In the loins from which he once was born*
> *He later quenches his passionate lust.*
> *She who was his mother shall be his wife,*
> *And his wife shall be his mother.*
> *His father shall become his son,*
> *And his son shall again become his father.*
>
> *Thus, in the cycles of samsara,*
> *Like scoops upon a whirling water-wheel,*
> *He is born from a mother's womb*
> *Again, again and yet again.*

Assuming that the thesis I presented earlier are indeed true, it would seem that, at the beginning of time, there were genderless (or androgynous) souls who, either in the course of the plunge into dualistic matter or in the course of cosmic evolution, somehow became divided into two parts, one male and one female. As a mental exercise, let us consider the case of Sam and Sara. I have chosen these names to represent all soul mates since, taken together, these two familiar English names yield a pun on the cycle of reincarnations, known in Sanskrit as "*samsara.*" This play on words is particularly appropriate, of course, because the division of the dyad (at least into the separate bodies we see today) was precipitated by the fall into samsara! In their first incarnation after they were split apart, Sam and Sara came to Earth as two separate individuals, but each was essentially identical with the other and, as a mundane reflection of the fact that they belonged to one another completely, Sam and Sara met, married and lived together as a loving couple (see also Genesis 4:1). This same pattern may well have been repeated throughout many incarnations, and we can even assume that Sam and Sara retained their original genders and perhaps even their same names throughout each of these many rebirths (see also Genesis 4:25).

After some time had gone by, it chanced that in a later incarnation Sam (as Jack) and Sara (as Mary) met again. (The name changes have been introduced to clarify, in an allegorical sense, the fact that they have now "finally" and completely slipped into the power of matter and must live in "darkness" from now on.) Once again, they met, married and lived as a couple. This time, however Sam (as Jack) did not treat Sara (as Mary) as an equal because Jack believed that a man was more worthwhile than a woman. Later, Sam was reincarnated as Cindy and Sara as John. Once again they met, married and lived together as a couple, but this time their gender roles were reversed. Once again, their marriage was fraught with differences of opinion about the value of the genders.

Later, and for the first time, Sam and Sara experienced an incarnation in which each remained unmarried and alone because they never met one another. For the first time, their lives were burdened by a profound sorrow. Despite all their searching, they simply could not find one another. Other re-incarnations followed: sometimes Sam as a man and Sara as a woman, sometimes vice versa, but in each lifetime they found and fell in love with one another. Once again, their lives together were marred by strife and squabbles, so that in the following incarnation they were prevented from meeting one another. Their originally pure love for one another had become so shallow and each of them had fallen so deeply into the ignorance of the material realm that Sam now decided to marry a "stranger" named Barbara and Sara decided to marry a "stranger" named Kevin. These marriages marked the first so-called "partner swap" for Sam and Sara. Sam didn't miss Sara nor did Sara miss Sam; both of them were content to enjoy the new friendships they had found in their new spouses. But Sam's relationship to Barbara and Sara's relationship to Kevin were not infused with the same deep intimacy that had characterized the loves they had originally known with their soul mates.

For all these reasons, Sam and Sara were prevented from meeting one another again throughout several subsequent incarnations. When they did chance to meet, they did not always become a loving couple. Sometimes one of them, sometimes the other, and sometimes both of them would find another person more interesting, and their affection for each other would remain strictly platonic. Then there might come incarnations in which both seemed not to be "made for one another," despite the fact that they actually had been made for one another since the beginning of time. The reason for this is that some interspersed incarnations have purposes that are diametrically opposed to the laws of eternity. During these embodiments, they may have been close friends of the same gender, father and daughter, mother and son, or else they might equally well have been incarnated as mother and daughter, father and son, and so on. In later lifetimes they might have been brother and sister, brother and brother, sister and sister, or else have been related to one another in whatever combinations one cares to imagine.

To sum things up, we can conclude that all souls share the same origin and are thus absolutely equal in value, regardless of which bodies they happen to inhabit and which genders they exhibit during the present incarnation. The Gospel According to St. John and the Brihadaranyaka Upanishad both confirm this statement (see Chapter One). Prabhupada expresses this wisdom in highly significant words: "The spiritual soul is equally pure in every incarnation, but those who do not possess adequate intelligence see only physical differences, like the differences between animals and humans."[11]

Since the soul is neither a plant nor an animal nor yet a human being (because the soul is divine), it should not be difficult to comprehend that the soul is also neither male nor female. The dual-souls doctrine need not contradict this view since the two souls who encounter one another after they have entered the physical realm were originally united as a complete, androgynous human. Apart yet created for one another, one half now embodies the masculine and the other half the feminine principle. In the most favorable situation, soul mates confront one another in bodies of opposite genders; they fall in love and live together as a loving couple. But soul mates can also fail to encounter one another or, if they do meet, can enter into other types of relationships with one another. For example, they can meet as individuals of the same gender, and develop a close friendship if the circumstance are favorable. Or an unhealthy rivalry can develop. This type of combination helps explain the genesis of homosexual relationships, but by no means justifies such liaisons. In most cases, a same-gender relationship precludes sexual interaction. Nor is a sexual relationship legitimate when soul mates incarnate as siblings or as parent and child. Likewise illegitimate is an adulterous relationship that arises when soul mates meet after one or both has already entered into other serious commitments. Most of these combinations inevitably result in some sort of disorder or disruption. Nowadays, unfortunately, *disturbed relationships* of this type seem to be the rule rather than the exception. The most common disturbance is probably that which results when soul mates go through their lives without ever encountering one another.

5. ABOUT MUNDANE AND

CELESTIAL MARRIAGES

Just as the material world must be modeled after a primal spiritual principle (see Chapter One), so, too, must earthly marriages (or common-law marriages that offer intimacy equal to that of officially wedded couples) be patterned after some celestial model. At this point I would like to expressly state that this book (and especially the following chapter) uses the words "marriage" or "partnership" to describe all types of living together. On the one hand, common-law marriages ought to be regarded as bonafide marriages; on the other hand, a marriage is also a partnership since it is only truly a marriage if both partners feel they are each other's spouses. A marriage is consummated when both souls feel they are inwardly united, even if they have not been externally married in an official ceremony conducted by a member of the clergy or a justice of the peace. At the same time, a marriage with all the trappings of consummation (including a marriage certificate) is not really consummated unless each spouse feels an inner bond uniting the couple. Anyone who has married merely for money cannot expect to live with his or her spouse in a genuine marriage, although an authentic marital relationship could develop over time. The pattern, or primordial idea, on which mundane marriages are based is the so-called "heavenly" or "celestial" marriage (i.e., a communal partnership between two soul mates made for one another since the beginning of time.

In the following statement, Jesus seems to disagree with this view of marriage: "There are some eunuchs who were so born from their mother's womb. And there are some eunuchs who were made eunuchs of men. And there are eunuchs who have made themselves eunuchs for the kingdom of heaven's sake. He that is able to receive it, let him receive it." (Matthew 19:12)

80   After we have grasped the true meaning of this verse, we will see that Jesus is not really opposed to marriage. However, in order to understand this, we must first clear up some potential misunderstandings. The phrase declaring that some men have "made themselves eunuchs for the kingdom of heaven's sake" seems to suggest that the practice of celibacy is the path that leads men back to God. We must look more deeply if we are to discern the real meaning behind these words. It is clear that marriage, as such, cannot be against God's will, since God Himself created woman after He saw that "it is not good that man should be alone" (see Genesis 2:18).

By entering into the partnership between husband and wife, man and woman are no longer two, but again become "one flesh" (see Genesis 2:24). The more spiritual these partners are, the more deeply they are able to experience their marriage as a spiritual union. Partners whose interests are directed more toward the mundane realm are more apt to compete with one another and tend to remain two distinct and different individuals. They cannot achieve oneness because they have not evolved far enough within themselves. Their goals are egotistical, either because they need to feel superior to their partners or because they are afraid of feeling inferior to their partners. Whether through arrogance or through fear, the result is the same: both partners stay isolated within themselves and each remains a mere half rather than part of a whole. Spiritually advanced partners, on the other hand, ascend into higher spiritual spheres and merge spiritually to become a single entity. This union need not always occur physically, although it can take the form of loving embrace or sexual intercourse. I will discuss this spiritual union and its analogous physical union in greater detail in Chapter Seven.

Spiritually advanced partners do not keep themselves aloof from the rest of creation, but strive to serve the entire cosmos. Mahatma Gandhi's marriage is a good example of this. Spiritually evolved souls experience themselves as existing in unity with the entire cosmos and with all beings. Of course, an unmarried individual can do good deeds that benefit society and all sentient beings but, as a rule, an unmarried person's energies are more quickly exhausted. A spiritual partnership, on the other hand, is like a self-recharging battery whose two poles continually motivate one another to perform new deeds of philanthropy and benevolence.

As we demonstrated in Chapter One, the sole complete and perfect image of God is the entity who is created and described in the first chapter of the Book of Genesis. Only this dyadic being truly deserves to be called "human." People who arose after the division of the genders described in Genesis 2 only deserve the appellation "human" when they are considered together (i.e., in combination with their complementary souls). Earthly "humans" are either men or women, and are therefore necessarily incomplete, imperfect and in need of completion through the opposite gender. According to Swedenborg, this cannot be otherwise because "the differentiation of the two genders, and the interaction between them, reflect a primal law of creation."[1]

The *Revelations of Ramala* agrees: "To know the true meaning of marriage, we must return to the beginning of creation, to that point in cosmic evolution when individuals were created. At this moment of cosmic creation, your spirit was divided into two aspects, into the duality of positive and negative, masculine and feminine."[2]

The authors continue in the same vein: "If a person lives in isolation, he or she can only bring forth things that reflect his or her own consciousness—and, thus, only half of creation, either the male or female half. But, if a person lives in a harmonious marriage, if he or she lives together with someone who embodies the other half of creation in its divine aspect, then two creative energies can unite to become a harmonious and balanced whole."[3]

82   Bo Yin Ra also writes about the deeper meaning of marriage and lends support to the hypothesis I presented at the beginning of this chapter: "Blessed are they who, married in this earthly life, have found their own eternal counterpart, the opposite pole with whom they ought to remain eternally united in spirit as a communal dyad and with whom they were once united prior to the binary division!"[4]

From what has just been said, we can see that a person only truly becomes human through his or her counterpart (i.e., a man through his wife and a woman through her husband). We can also see that earthly partnership is a reflection of the love that exists between soul mates and is surely not a transgression against God's will. Not until the New Testament do we find certain passages that, at first reading, would seem to council against marriage. The Old Testament and the Books of the Apocrypha contain nothing but positive statements about the value of marriage. For example, verse 18:22 in the *Proverbs of Solomon* says: "Whoso findeth a wife findeth a good thing, and obtaineth favor of the Lord."

An apocryphal text called *The Book of Sirach* contains the following words: "The man who takes a wife has the makings of a fortune, a helper who suits him and a pillar on which to lean." (36:26) Although these wise words are directed toward men, they apply, of course, to women as well.

It is commonly believed that Jesus never married, a fact that might lead some Christians to follow his example and conclude (against the tradition of the Old Testament) that life as a bachelor or bachelorette is preferable to married life for those who have chosen the spiritual path. Paul seems to support this view in his first epistle to the Corinthians: "It is good for a man not to touch a woman. Nevertheless, to avoid fornication, let every man have his own wife, and let every woman have her own husband." (First Corinthians 7:1-2) But, in the seventh verse of this same chapter, Paul makes it clear that this advice represents only his own personal opinions about marriage and celibacy: "For I would that all men were even as I myself. But every man hath his proper gift of God, one after this manner and another after that."

All of us have our own God-given gifts, our personal mission in life, our special destiny in each particular incarnation. Thus, marriage or a similarly intimate partnership is intended for some people, while others are fated to remain alone. Those who are fated to remain without a partner, but who nonetheless yearn for an enduring love relationship, can console themselves with the knowledge that the time for such a partnership has not arrived. They must first fulfill some task (dharma), which they should perform joyfully, without succumbing to self-pity about being single. If they can achieve this, new horizons will no doubt appear in due course. When the time is ripe, and after they have performed their destined tasks, the appropriate partner will surely arrive on schedule. Being alone can also have other karmic causes—for example, because one abandoned one's partner in a past incarnation and must now "do penance" for that past cruelty. *Penance*, we should realize, means nothing more nor less than *rethinking our situation.*

Divyanand agrees with this view: "Our live is largely determined by our earlier karma, by the deeds we did during our previous lifetimes. Although we make many decisions according to our own free will, our entire lives must nonetheless remain within certain fated limits. These boundaries have been drawn around us prior to our births and we cannot escape them. Whether a person will marry or remain single is determined according to that person's karma and in accord with the will of God....If God

has willed that a certain person must live an unmarried life because of his or her past karma or spiritual background, that individual will eventually realize this fact from within and from his
or her own motivation."[5]

According to Paul's rather peculiar formulation (in First
Corinthians 7:2), he regards the sole meaning and purpose of
marriage as an expedient *to avoid fornication.* At this point I
want to unequivocally express my disagreement with Paul's view
and state that the real meaning and purpose of marriage does not
lie in satisfying or indulging our sexual lusts. Since Paul views
the institution of marriage solely as a playground for the satisfaction of base lusts, he prefers to live alone. Paul is quite clear
on this point when he writes: "I say, therefore, to the unmarried
and widows, it is good for them if they abide as I. But if they
cannot contain, let them marry: for it is better to marry than to
burn." (First Corinthians 7:8-9)

Sexual intercourse on Earth is modeled after the union of two
loving soul mates that takes place in higher spiritual spheres
(see Chapter Seven). Sexual love cannot be characterized as
sinful. This assumes, of course, it is motivated by the sole
proper motivation—namely, the mutual desire for physical and
spiritual unification that culminates in the wish to surrender
ourselves entirely to our beloved and become a single entity,
together with the beloved, throughout all eternity. In other
words, the decisive factor is whether the motivation for sexual
intercourse stems from the heart or from the loins. Is the love
felt by both of the two partners so strong that they desire nothing more ardently than to merge their hearts and souls? Or is it
merely lust and physical appearance that fuel the desire for
sexual activity, and is the partner's identity irrelevant or even
interchangeable? We can conclude that, when sexuality is
grounded in the context of a harmonious and lasting partnership, sexual union can represent a peak experience within that
partnership. If, on the other hand, the sexual act is divorced
from an enduring partnership and performed merely to satisfy

physical lusts and base desires, it is without spiritual value and can be described as sinful.

Plato's ideas about this agree with mine. In *Symposium*, for example, Pausanias declares: "Every action is of the following sort: when done in terms of itself, it is neither noble nor base....If it is done correctly, it proves to be noble, and if done incorrectly, base. So, too, in the case of loving and Eros, for Eros itself is neither noble nor deserving of a eulogy, but only if Eros provokes one to love in a noble way is Eros noble." At a later point in his discourse, Pausanias adds: "It is neither noble nor base in itself, but if nobly done, noble, and if basely done, base....It is the pandemian lover who is no good, the one in love with the body rather than the soul. He is not even a lasting lover, because he is in love with a thing that is not lasting. As soon as the bloom of the body fades—which is what he was in love with—he is off and takes wing, having made a foul shame of many speeches and promises. But he who is in love with a good character remains throughout life, for he is welded to what is lasting."

Let us take a closer look at Paul's words in the 27th, 32nd and 33rd verses of the seventh chapter of First Corinthians. "Art thou bound unto a wife? Seek not to be loosed. Art thou loosed from a wife? Seek not a wife." (7:27) "But I would have you without carefulness. He who is unmarried careth for the things that belong to the Lord, how he may please the Lord." (7:32) "But he who is married careth for the things that are of the world, how he may please his wife." (7:33)

According to the dual-souls doctrine and the spiritual love between man and woman, the yearning of one soul for its primordial Thou is the greatest, most intense yearning possible, second only to the soul's yearning for God. In *Symposium*, Plato agrees that the soul experiences an ardent yearning to reunite with its counterpart. The Bible also recognizes the awesome might of this yearning that impels a man "to leave his father and his mother, and...cleave unto

his wife: and they shall be one flesh." (Genesis 2:24) The apparent
contradiction between this and First Corinthians 7:27, in which it is
written that an unmarried man should "seek not a wife," can be re-
solved when we realize that this passage only means that neither
men nor women should dissipate their energies in "the pursuit of
happiness." This is because, if it is appropriate for our destiny, the
predetermined partner for this incarnation (who is not necessarily
our dual soul) will, sooner or later, naturally appear. There is no need
for a lengthy and elaborate search. Conversely, we can search in-
tensely for a person with whom to establish an enduring relationship, but if such a partnership is not appropriate for our current
karma or for this incarnation, that search will not meet with success.
A fruitless search for a soul mate or for some other partner only dis-
tracts us from our spiritual quest.

First Corinthians 7:27 further suggests that we ought to be satisfied with what we already have. We ought to accept our present
partnership, our position in professional life, our possessions,
and so on. Paul's words also mean that we should not waste time
with idle speculations about how to change things. Rather, it is
important to learn to cope with current circumstances. All our
unrequited wishes and useless woes only cause headaches, sorrow, dissatisfaction and suffering. We must realize that whatever we have and whatever we lack are the consequences of our
own karma. If we are not prepared to accept this, we will easily
stray from the spiritual path, and become dissatisfied and inex-
tricably entangled in worldly affairs.

The 32nd and 33rd verses in chapter seven of First Corinthians
are only an insinuation, since it is not the married person but the
one without a partner, or the one who is searching for an appropriate partner, who is most likely to occupy his or her attention
with mundane affairs, especially because he or she is eager to
please the opposite sex. On the other hand, a happily married
person who has already found a partner for life is free from this
burden and can concentrate his or her energies on pursuing the
spiritual path. Of course, this attempt to refute Paul's insinua-

tion is itself only an assumption. It presumes that the person who has no partner is searching for one and further presumes that people who live together as couples have dedicated themselves to a mutual search for spiritual realization. It should be clear, then, that not all biblical verses are equally significant, although some "Bible thumping" Christians who cling too doggedly to literal readings and fail to grasp the deeper meaning beneath the words would have us believe otherwise. What Paul is trying to say here is this: as a rule, a married man (or woman) is more likely to be occupied with worldly matters because of his (or her) duties and responsibilities to spouse and family; an unmarried person is responsible only to himself (or herself) and to God and is thus less likely to become entangled in mundane affairs. We have seen, however, that since all these arguments are based on unproven assumptions, they cannot serve as the basis for any universally valid conclusions and thus in no way cast aspersions upon, or reduce the value of, spiritual marriage.

Jesus' words in Matthew 19:12 (cited earlier), as well as the passage in First Corinthians 7:27, mean that we should not allow ourselves to become unduly distracted by sublunary affairs. A partnership will inevitably have a mundane component whenever one partner is more spiritually oriented and the other more worldly, since the spiritual partner will not be able to pursue the yearning for God in the same measure as he (or she) could if he (or she) had stayed single or if his (or her) partner were likewise spiritually inclined. The worldly partner in a relationship of this sort is likely to exert a negative influence that burdens the relationship and hinders the spiritual progress of the spouse. However, since two such people have found one another because of their shared karma, a positive influence could flow from the more spiritually inclined partner toward the more worldly one.

The main reason for the advice not to marry is surely because, in biblical times no less than today, people have seldom been able to distinguish love from passion. They have always tended to indulge their passions rather than lead lives of genuine love free from egotism, jealousy and similar vices. The spirituality of both partners is an essential component in a complete *dyadic partnership*. The partnership can only fulfill its true purpose when the marital relationship is conducted in a spiritual manner—that is, when it is directed toward God, toward the spiritual progress of each partner and for the benefit of the community. Since spiritual people who dedicate themselves to God have always been few and far between, the advice in Matthew 19:12 is meant to warn spiritual individuals who are without partners that their search for an appropriate partner (perhaps even for a "phantom" partner) is apt to unnecessarily dissipate their energies and distract them from their quest for God and for the meaning and purpose of life. Only a spiritual partnership is a valuable partnership. Every other partnership (and, unfortunately, there are a great many liaisons of this sort) is worse than remaining single. Of course, staying single only makes sense when an unmarried person dedicates his (or her) energies to the spiritual quest.

The ideal relationship consists of two spiritual partners who, in living together, dedicate their lives to God and mutually support and encourage one another on their spiritual paths. A partnership of this kind is extraordinarily valuable from a spiritual point of view, since it empowers each spouse to achieve greater spiritual progress than he or she would have been able to achieve if that person had remained unmarried. As I have already explained in my commentary on Genesis 2:24 and in reference to the Vissells' conclusions, the synergy of two harmoniously intermingling creative energies is much greater than the sum of two separate parts. As we have seen, the skeptical attitude that some biblical verses take toward marriage is related above all to the sexual acts that might be involved in that marriage. If we consider these same biblical verses in the light of a spiritual partnership in which sexuality is not indulged in from lustful motives but is woven into the fabric of a harmonious relationship, then marriage takes on an entirely different quality. The authors of the Bible would surely agree that such a marriage is beneficial. Ideally, both partners should be involved in a spiritual quest, neither partner should feel restricted in his or her development and neither partner should feel dependent upon the other. I use the word "dependent" here to describe a situation in which both partners rely on one another for support, in which neither knows how to live on his or her own and in which each feels "worthless" because a vacuum is created the instant the other partner is absent. This negative dependency is all the more acute when one partner is "permanently" absent as a consequence of separation, divorce or death.

When a spouse dies, it is only natural for the bereaved to miss the beloved and to suffer grief. At such times, we should remember that everything that is born is subject to death, that dying is nothing unusual or out of the ordinary, that the process of dying is no more unusual than the process of falling asleep at night and that life continues for each of us. Profound grief after the loss of a partner is not evidence of excessive attachment; grief only becomes morbid when it weighs so heavily upon the survivor that it robs him or her of the will to live. Shakespeare expresses this realization most eloquently in *Romeo and Juliet* (III, v.): "Some grief shows much of love, but much of grief shows still some want of wit."

Another interesting issue in the context of the dual-souls doctrine concerns the nature of angels. In commentaries written by Christian theologians, we frequently read that angels are components of God and members of God's family in the truest sense. Since this description is not quite adequate for us here, I would like to investigate two other possibilities. As I do so, we ought to bear in mind that love is the highest commandment of every religion, and is the ultimate, universal gift that every human being is most happy to receive. It must, therefore, also be the case that redeemed souls experience love in the highest measure. This love can be the affection shared by soul mates—who, as angels, are once again male-female (see Chapter Seven)—or it can be the love experienced by each genderless angel as God's immediate beloved.

If the first possibility were the case, then the angels would represent the union of man and woman into the single entity that they were at the beginning (see Genesis 1:27) before the two halves were separated from each other (see Genesis 2:22). According to this theory, the redeemed souls would no longer need to marry one another since God has united the two separate parts into a single whole. This unification, enacted by God with the consent of the soul mates, is a different process than that which takes place in a mundane marriage. Since death puts an end to all earthly partnerships (which need not necessarily mean that the two entities will not encounter one another after death or in their next incarnations), and since earthly marriages can be dissolved by divorce, we see that the union of soul mates is a much more comprehensive and far-reaching process. Once reunited, they can never be separated again, nor do they wish to separate. Rather, they are delighted to be a single entity again and, within themselves, are sufficiently developed to know that they must never again endure the suffering they were compelled to undergo during their sojourn in matter when they spent most of their time separated. According to the Sohar, only this *whole* human, who is simultaneously male and female, deserves to be called "human" in the sense intended by Genesis 1:27, in which it is written that human beings were created "male and female." In this context, *to be whole* does not mean that two beings are united in such a way that both lose their own individuality, but means instead that they merge together *as one*. They remain two beings, but they experience themselves as *one unity*.

We can find confirmation for this theory in Swedenborg's writings. He claims that, during one of his spiritual flights into the heavens, an angel, accompanied by its dual soul, said to him: "We are one, her life is in me, my life is in her. We are two figures, but one soul."[6] It is for this reason that, in heaven, "two spouses are not called two angels, but one."[7]

We find additional corroboration for this theory in both the gnostic system of Markos and in the Koran. Sura 81:8 contains the following phrase in a report about the end of time: "When souls shall be paired with their bodies." This is a highly significant statement about the ultimate temporally and evolutionarily determined reunification of soul mates. Markos' gnostic system expresses a similar idea: "The redeemed lay aside their souls,...are raised up, led into the bridal chamber and surrendered unto their beloved."[8]

Emanuel Swedenborg describes the world of angels in the following words: "The goal of the creation of the universe is to allow an angelic heaven to exist (i.e., a realm of authentic counterparts, of genuine humans [in the sense of Genesis 1:27], of whom heaven is formed). The human race is heaven's botanical nursery."

However, Emanuel Swedenborg does not know all there is to know about the spiritual world. Although he reports that God can unite two compatible souls with one another and that this is the goal of human striving for perfection, he seems to be unaware that these unified souls (as long as we are not dealing with a karmically determined union but are witnessing the union of two souls who have belonged together since the beginning of time) already formed one entity in the past and that each of these souls originally came forth from that primordial unified entity. Likewise worth mentioning as evidence of his incomplete knowledge are his denial of the idea of reincarnation and his statement that the souls of animals do not continue to exist after their physical deaths. We should read his reports without prejudice, especially because they sound reasonable and enlightening, but we should by no means accept them as absolute truth without subjecting them to thorough examination.

This leads us to a fundamental spiritual principle that is most cogently expressed by Buddha: "Do not believe in mere hearsay, nor in traditions simply because they are ancient and have come down to us through many generations....That which you have determined through your own experience and investigations and reason and that which serves your own well-being and

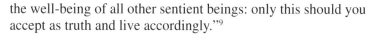

the well-being of all other sentient beings: only this should you accept as truth and live accordingly."[9]

Prabhupada's opinion about angels agrees with Swedenborg: "There are kisses and embraces in the spiritual world, but there is no satisfaction of the senses as there is in the material world."[10]

It seems likely that the beginning is always similar to the end. This parallelism leads us to ask about the nature of the angelic, heavenly state. Assuming that the first human was created as an androgynous being (see Genesis 1: 27), who combined male and female in one entity, we ought to regard this primal human as the most ancient image for which biblical testimony exists. But is it not true that everything that was once created, even if it continues to exist for eons, must someday necessarily pass out of existence? According to the Bible, the androgynous human was created, so we must ask ourselves *of what* was that human created? Was the primordial hermaphrodite formed from a higher, never created— and therefore eternal—male-female image or from a genderless entity? Or was the primal human created in some other manner of which we have no knowledge? Is the ultimate and final state the same as that which existed prior to the creation of the primal hermaphrodite described in Genesis 1:27? Why does the Bible tell us nothing about this prior state? Or is the final state of humankind identical with that of the primal hermaphrodite? Would not this androgynous entity languish alone and suffer the pangs of loneliness? Or is the final state the same as that which existed prior to the binary division: a state of genuine counterparts who exist with and for one another? After all, these two entities must have lived happily together before they sinned.

The first hypothesis posits either a union of two entities—one male, the other female—into a single androgynous being (as in Genesis 1:27) or else a counterpart entity (as in Genesis 2:18). In the preceding paragraph I presented some unanswered questions that raise doubts about the correctness of this hypothesis. Of what substance was this androgynous human (in Genesis 1:27) created? After what spiritual image was it patterned? Unfortunately, I cannot answer these questions and, at best, could only add more possible hypotheses—a task I feel is best left undone.

We can, however, be sure that turning away from all mundane phenomena is the goal of life espoused by Christian, Hindu and Buddhist scriptures alike. This rejection of mundane concerns specifically includes a turning away from our life companion. In Luke 18:29-30, Jesus declares: "Verily I say unto you, 'There is no man that hath left house, or parents, or brethren, or wife or children for the kingdom of God's sake, who shall not receive manifold more in this present time, and in the world to come of life everlasting.'"

It is only natural to wonder how leaving our families, for whom we ought to be responsible, could possibly be an expression of divine will. Here, again, we have raised a question I cannot answer. I can only imagine that a person who has already advanced this far along the spiritual path would instinctively know that God will provide for his (or her) family. I want to emphasize that actually leaving our families is by no means necessary. The verse under scrutiny here does not mean that we should abandon our homes and families, but only that we ought to place more importance upon God than upon our families and that we should love God even more deeply than we love our own families. Jesus explains: "He that loveth father or mother more than me is not worthy of me: and he that loveth son or daughter more than me is not worthy of me." (Matthew 10:37) A parable can help us understand this message more clearly. Suppose a man were married to a woman who constantly asked her mother for advice, and who followed that advice even when it ran contrary to her husband's wishes. It is obvious that the wife in this case feels more akin to her mother than her husband. She has not "cut the umbilical cord" that binds her to her mother and, thus, cannot be an adequate partner for her husband. She need not spurn her mother, nor sever all ties to her. Just as this woman needs to turn away from her mother and toward her husband so, too, must we turn away from our families and turn our attention toward God.

If we follow these religious notions about leaving our families or becoming homeless—or at least turning away from our families on an inner plane for the sake of God—we might be led to believe that reunification with God is the soul's only goal. Dissolution of all familial bonds, including ties to our spouse or life companion, almost sounds like a contradiction of the dual-souls doctrine. From our previous discussion, we know for certain that soul mates exist. But could it nonetheless be true that soul mates no longer exist at that time when the entities finally return to nirvana? Could it be that the entities cast off everything—including their souls—before they enter that ultimate state? Since the soul is without gender, and since the Self (the spirit of God) that animates that soul is surely without gender (or else represents the latent unity of both genders within itself), it seems likely that, if we follow this theory to its logical conclusion, the Self would no longer need any link between soul mates. Since every entity (i.e., every Self) is complete within itself, it would seem that the male-female polarity is only active within the confines of our limited awareness.

We are fairly certain that the soul possesses no permanent gender and that it freely takes on bodies of one or the other gender during its various incarnations. For this reason, people who ascribe to the *evolutive* principle (see the explanation in the preceding chapter) argue that the perfect human being is neither a man nor a woman, but a person who harmoniously unites both gender principles in one body. According to adherents of the evolutive principle, this transcendent union of gender characteristics is the goal of all evolution. If we follow this thesis (which declares that the eternal linkage between soul mates is illusory), we can propose the following hypothesis as an alternative to the first theory.

First of all, we must abandon the idea that a life without love between men and women cannot be worth living. This may be difficult to imagine since, to our mundane minds, the loving union of the genders represents the greatest possible bliss, even though we know that mundane love also has a few (and frequently more than just a few) negative aspects. If love between the genders were to come to an end, there would have to be another, much more valuable and blissful love to replace it. Such a love is indeed conceivable within the context of this hypothesis, because the soul is *God's beloved* and the bliss that God's love brings to the soul far exceeds the transitory pleasures derived from any other love relationship.

When an individual being feels itself drawn into the indescribable embrace of God's all-encompassing love, that individual experiences ultimate bliss. This joy is everlasting since it is without temporal limits. Nothing but the repetition of the fall from grace could put an end to it. However, as I mentioned earlier with regard to soul mates, a relapse into sin would be unthinkable since only redeemed souls—all of whom have already realized that mundane joys are ultimately illusory—attain nirvana. They have left the duality (and the suffering associated with that duality) of the material world behind. Since they know all this, it seems unlikely that redeemed souls would be in danger of lapsing into duality or sin. This view is supported by Buddha's realization and by Hindu philosophy: "For him who has once reached nirvana, there is no further return to the material world." The difference between the fall from grace and the purely theoretical danger of a relapse into sin is that the entities who committed the original sin, as described in the Bible, had not learned to differentiate between *good and evil*. This is not the case for entities who subsequently achieve redemption. These latter redeemed ones possess an all-encompassing realization, and take care to avoid repeating such a serious error, especially since they know from experience that the suffering that ensues from sin is all-encompassing and dreadfully long-lasting.

God's all-embracing love (which I described in the preceding paragraphs) enables the souls (or however else one chooses to name the redeemed entities) to experience ultimate bliss. This joy is so delightful that they never want to lose it. God's love is free from every sorrow, strife or similar misfortune. The redeemed entities are so fully absorbed in divine love that they have no reason to feel jealous or to doubt the righteousness of this love. In fact, such redeemed beings are already entirely free of such human weaknesses as jealousy or doubt. The bliss that they experience is indescribable; our finite minds are incapable of conceiving it. As long as we remain attached to our bodies, we can never be entirely free and, thus, cannot enjoy omniscience or omnipotence. As we penetrate further into spiritual spheres, our sense of well-being, security and comfort increases correspondingly.

Divyanand lends his support to this second hypothesis, that posits a union of souls with divinity, in the following words: "To separate the soul or the consciousness of a human being from the body, to transport that soul into the realm of spirit and lead it back to God—these are tasks that no earthly wife can perform. They can only be enacted by the divine spouse—the stream of divine revelations."[11]

The two aforementioned hypotheses—whether soul mates merge with one another or whether a merger of the souls with God takes place—are questionable, since they contradict one another. A third possibility would be to combine and reconcile the two hypotheses: soul mates merge with one another, yet at the same time they are absorbed into God's all-encompassing love. This third hypothesis asserts the *trinity* of creation. Just as earthly couples concentrate on the creation of a third being in the form of a child, so spiritual partners consummate their union through merging with one another and with God.

We need to decide which of these three hypotheses is correct. After considering this theme for a long time, I now believe that only the third hypothesis can be correct. I will explain my reasons for this belief in the following paragraphs.

If the first hypothesis were true, would that mean that all the statements derived from the second hypothesis would nec-

essarily be false? Conversely, if the second hypothesis were
true, would all the conclusions based on the first hypothesis
necessarily be false? But are not both these hypotheses incomplete? So the third hypothesis must be the correct one,
since it represents the union and reconciliation of the two
foregoing hypotheses. The first hypothesis is correct in its
description of the merging of soul mates (the union of the
masculine and feminine aspects), but it is incomplete because it does not explicitly include the merging of these souls
with God. The second hypothesis suffers from similar flaws:
it, too, is partly correct yet incomplete since, although it
describes the merging of the souls with God, it does not discuss the merging of soul mates with one another. Thus, it
ignores the re-establishment of the holistic state of being
enjoyed by the original hermaphroditic human prior to its
division, as described in Genesis 2:21ff.

The third hypothesis rectifies the deficits of the first two and
complements them both in a nearly ideal manner. This third hypothesis confirms the idea of an essential parallelism between
the beginning and the end, and posits a development that moves
in precisely the reverse direction from the one described in Genesis 1:27 and 2:21ff, in which the story of the creation of humanity is told. The holistic male-female human first emanated
from God (Genesis 1:27), then later divided into two genders.
(Genesis 2:21ff) The events along the return path would necessarily occur in exactly the opposite order. The beings would first
overcome the separation of the genders (through reunification
of each entity with its corresponding dual soul). Then the newly
reunited male-female entities would unite with God in the so-
called *unio mystica*.

The fact that a particular soul has already attained a very high
state of spiritual evolution does not mean that it will encounter
its dual soul during this earthly incarnation. Even a spiritually
evolved soul might have to wait until its energies and those of
its dual were liberated. This liberation occurs when the souls

leave their bodies at death. These deaths could occur simultaneously but at separate places on Earth. Once freed of their earthly bodies, soul mates are finally free to meet on the astral plane at the threshold of heaven, where, at long last, they merge with one another and enter into nirvana as one.

To conclude our discussion of these three hypotheses, and to add extra emphasis to the third theory, we should recall that Jesus' statement in Luke 20:34-36 neither confirms nor denies the dual-souls doctrine. We should also consider the fact that Jesus never denied the idea (as described in Genesis) that both man and woman arose from the binary fission of an originally holistic hermaphrodite. Bearing in mind the other traditions (e.g., the Sohar, Plato's *Symposium* and the various myths we discussed in Chapter Two), we can conclude that the dual-souls doctrine is not in error. Of course, some people believe that the biblical tale of the division of the primal human does not refer to the creation of man and woman *per se*, but should be understood allegorically as a description of the creation of the *inner* and *outer* (or *astral* and *physical*) human beings. Although this allegorical interpretation has its merits, it cannot explain the creation of woman as a direct consequence of the realization that "it is not good that man should be alone; I will make him an help meet for him." (Genesis 2:18)

Our discussion in this chapter has gotten a bit ahead of itself, since I want to reserve my comments about nirvana for Chapter Eight. In this present chapter, I will restrict myself to a discussion of the nature of the angels (i.e., the ultimate, lasting constitution of living beings).

In a certain sense, Jesus' words in Luke 20:35-36 refer to the astral plane where souls dwell during the interval between incarnations. Here, too, matrimony does not exist, although we can assume that the souls feel affection for one another of the sort I discussed in relation to the first hypothesis about the world of angels. Neither is there sexual intercourse or reproduction here since, if immortal souls were to multiply themselves, the number of souls would increase infinitely.

It seems likely that Emanuel Swedenborg actually penetrated into the astral realm and that his statements (which I discussed in this chapter) are indeed eyewitness reports from that region. But Swedenborg does not seem to have been aware of nirvana, since that knowledge is reserved for fully evolved, completely perfected beings.

To close this chapter, I would like to briefly discuss the nature of the astral realm.

First, we know that immediately after we die, our souls are met and received by the souls of people whom we loved on Earth and who died before us. In many cases, the newly departed individual sees a being of light. This luminous figure is often identified as Jesus Christ. Readers interested in a more detailed discussion of this theme are urged to consult literature by Raymond A. Moody and Elisabeth Kübler-Ross.

A Buddhist verse describes after-death experiences as follows: "When a traveler safely returns home from a long journey, his friends and relations greet him with joy. Just so, when a person who has lived righteously arrives in heaven, he is greeted by his own good deeds like relatives greeting a beloved friend."

The Bible also provides a number of clues about the world that awaits us after death. Here, however, I will mention only the well-known story about the rich man and the beggar Lazarus, since it sheds light on the differences between the coarse (material) world and the ethereal (astral) realm. This biblical tale (see Luke 16:19ff) tells of two men: a rich man who was "clothed in purple and fine linen and [who] fared sumptuously every day" and an indigent man named Lazarus who, his miserable body covered with sores, lay at the rich man's gate and begged "to be fed with the crumbs that fell from the rich man's table." When the poor man died, he "was carried by the angels" and laid "in Abraham's bosom." The rich man, on the other hand, went to hell and, in the midst of his torments, saw "Abraham afar off, and Lazarus in his bosom. And he cried and said, 'Father Abraham, have mercy on me, and send Lazarus that he may dip the tip of his finger in water and cool my tongue, for I am tormented in this flame.' But Abraham said, 'Son, remember that thou in thy lifetime receivest thy good things, and likewise Lazarus evil things. But now he is comforted, and thou art tormented.'"

According to this story, it seems entirely possible that a person who spends his or her earthly life yearning for a true beloved but who never meets that longed-for soul mate could ultimately be reunited with the dual soul after death and, like Lazarus, enjoy the blessings of an immeasurably blissful afterlife.

The following passage from Swedenborg's writings agrees with this view: "We know that, during the span of his earthly life, not every man meets the right partner or finds the mate with whom he is truly bound in a spiritual marriage." What matters most, according to Swedenborg, is "that the man knows about the proper goal of life, that he yearns for that goal and that he does not dissipate his energies longing for an earthly relationship, since he knows that neither he as a man alone, nor she as a woman alone, can ever be a complete human being."[13]

6. STORIES AND PARABLES

This chapter deals with stories that describe the love between soul mates, or at least that are characteristic of this love. Toward the end of the chapter, I will present two parables that shed light on the essence of soul mates.

PETER IBBETSON

The English author and caricaturist George Du Maurier was born on March 6, 1834 in Paris and died on October 8, 1896 in London. He was the grandfather of the writer Daphne Du Maurier. Among his other works, George Du Maurier wrote *Peter Ibbetson*, a short novel that contains an extraordinary description of the love that unites a pair of soul mates. I will retell that tale in rather lengthy detail, first because the book is hard to find and out of print (its most recent edition was printed in 1963 by The Heritage Press of New York) and second because of the profound esoteric insights—not solely about soul mates—that it contains. Furthermore, I believe that this most interesting and unfortunately largely forgotten narrative is an excellent example of a story about soul mates.

The story begins in Passy, a suburb of Paris, during the mid-nineteenth century. A little girl named Mimsey Seraskier and a boy named Pierre Pasquier de la Marière, nicknamed "Gogo," both live in the same neighborhood. Since their families live so close together, it is only natural for the two children to spend many carefree hours playing together, and both enjoy a wonderfully happy childhood. After the untimely death of Pierre's parents, a certain Colonel Ibbetson (a relative of Pierre's mother) arranges to have the boy brought to London. From this point on, Pierre's and Mimsey's paths diverge. Pierre takes his uncle's family name, and from then on calls himself Peter Ibbetson.

Many years later, Peter sees a young woman at a party. From that moment on, his life changes in a peculiar way. Peter watches as this fascinating stranger asks their hostess about him. He likewise asks a shy man, who, like Peter, is standing alone in a corner, about the mysterious woman. The loner tells him that the woman is named "The Duchess of Towers." Although Peter assumes that he will never again encounter this wonderful duchess and that he will surely never have an opportunity to get to know her, Cupid's arrow nonetheless strikes deep in his heart. He knows that she will embody the ideal woman in his lonely life. Throughout the ensuing weeks, the memory of the Duchess of Towers dominates his life. By day and by night, he continually sees her face in his mind's eye.

Some time later, Peter travels to Paris for a brief visit. Not without a certain nostalgic feeling, he returns to the familiar places of his childhood. In the window of a passing carriage, Peter chances to see the Duchess of Towers. Her gaze illuminates Peter Ibbetson like an unexpected sunbeam from heaven.

Still recalling every detail of her radiant face, Peter falls asleep that night in his hotel room and has a dream that marks the beginning of the first phase of his true inner life. In that dream, he again encounters the mysterious duchess, who speaks to him in a friendly manner. "Give me your hand," she says, "and come in here." Peter immediately feels that this is no ordinary dream, but is a miraculous and hitherto unknown event that transcends anything he has ever experienced in mere earthly life.

When Peter awakes from his dream, he does not feel the least bit more awake than he had felt himself to be a minute earlier. Indeed, he feels *less* awake! He can recall every detail of the dream experience. He knows that an ordinary dream is full of interruptions and discontinuities, and that it usually fades in a short time, leaving the dreamer with only a vague memory of what he dreamt. He thinks again about the "dream" he has just experienced, and realizes that it is free of such shortcomings. Just the opposite: all through the marvelous interval when he held her hand, Peter felt as though he had been absorbing her entire life into himself.

He returns to London, but feels that his life has been completely transformed. The ordinary day at work seems as irrelevant as a mere dream. His entire being is permeated by the memory of the Duchess of Towers, who has kindled an inner fire in him and brought his soul into harmony with itself and with all of humanity. His genuine life, Peter feels, only begins in the evenings when he goes to bed and prepares for his nightly dreams. He soon discovers that no friendship in waking life could ever be as intense as this liaison, and that no impressions received through his waking senses could possibly be as intense and as fulfilling as those he experiences during these peculiarly vivid dreams. Nightly encounters with the Duchess of Towers become a life within a life for him.

Peter soon receives another invitation from Lady Cray. Arriving at her home, he glimpses the Duchess of Towers a third time. Peter asks the man sitting beside him at dinner what this lady's maiden-name was. "She was a Miss Seraskier. They lived somewhere near Paris. It was there that Madame Seraskier [her mother] died of cholera." Peter Ibbetson nearly faints. He asks himself how it could be possible that he had failed to recognize that this enchanting young woman was none other than his childhood friend Mimsey. He does not dare to glance even fleetingly at her face throughout the remainder of the evening.

The next morning, when Peter once again encounters his beloved Duchess, she explains to him that, although she has learned that his name is Mr. Ibbetson, he nonetheless reminds her of a little French boy she had known during her childhood. Peter reveals that, indeed, many years ago, he really was that little French boy. She asks him what his childhood name was. When he answers, she turns pale and her whole body begins to tremble. Then he tells her about his first dream about her, and they realize that they both shared that dream with one another. Mary begins to feel uncertain and anxious. "We had better part now," she says. "I don't know if I shall ever meet you again....I will now say good-bye and leave you....That is best. I think this had better be a final adieu. I cannot tell you of what interest you are to me and always have been....We shall often think of each other—that is inevitable—*but never, never dream*....Dear Mr. Ibbetson, I wish you all the good that one human being can wish another. And now good-bye, and may God in heaven bless you!" The light fades from Peter's life, and he is left alone again—more miserable and more pitiful than he would have been if they had never met.

Although separated since childhood, neither had forgotten the other. Now they realize that a miraculous bond links them. This experience is so unprecedented that neither can ever disappear from the other's thoughts as long as life, the senses and their memories endure. Each is more conscious of the other's inner life than two mortals have ever been since the beginning of the world. And yet things turn out just as she predicted. After that final meeting, they never again meet one another, neither in waking life nor in their dreams, no matter how desperately they long for one another.

An entire year goes by. Then Peter Ibbetson's life is struck by a terrible catastrophe. Peter quarrels with his uncle and inadvertently kills him. He is convicted of murder and sentenced to life imprisonment. Feeling the need to explain things to the Duchess of Towers, he begins to write her a letter, but falls asleep while writing. And thus begins another phase in his inner life. Once again, the Duchess of Towers appears to him in a dream. While holding his hands in hers, she gazes into the depths of his heart, and finally says, "I could not understand why you should be in my dream, as I had almost always dreamt true....But it is still a mystery...that two people should meet as we are meeting now in one and the same dream....What a link between us, Mr. Ibbetson!" To prove that she was really sharing the very same dream with him, she promises to mail a letter to him in prison. The following day, he actually receives the promised missive. From that day on and for many years thereafter, they continue to rendezvous in their dreams almost every night.

What Peter and Mary shared were more than mere dreams. Their meetings, although incorporeal, were the quintessence of their lives. The reality of their link was complete and all-encompassing. Like twin nuts within a single shell, they were more closely linked than any other human couple, since every other individual lives, as it were, isolated within his or her own private shell. Although Mary and Peter grew quite old, in their dreams they remained perpetually youthful. Both seemed to stay about 28 years old. In waking life, time passed for them as it did for other people but, since their attention was so focused on their dream life, they were less aware of time's inexorable passage.

Finally the inevitable happens—Mary dies. Peter resolves to starve himself to death and refuses all nourishment, because Mary's death has left him bereft of all desire to live. Neither does he ever wish to dream again. But, despite this resolution, one evening he succumbs to a strange, nostalgic wish. He yearns to visit the sites of his childhood once more in a dream. He falls asleep and dreams once more but, in this dream, he is not young as he has always been in past dreams. His advanced age in this dream is identical with his actual age in waking life. The dream stroll through his childhood neighborhood is sad and sobering, and the heaviness of his heart is almost too much to bear. His heart is broken and his body is so weary that he can hardly keep himself moving. Never before has he felt weary within a dream. He drags himself to an ocean beach, where he finds a few scattered individuals, including one elderly woman sitting motionless on a bench. "Oh my God!" cries Peter. "It's Mary Seraskier!"

Mary explains to him: "Gogo, you have no idea how difficult it has been for me to come back, even for a few short hours, for I can't hold on very long. It is like hanging onto the window sill by one's wrists....Nobody has ever come back before....I have come a long way—such a long way—to have an *abboccamento* with you. I had so many things to say. But, now we are both here, hand-in-hand as we used to be, I can't even understand what they were. And, if I could, I couldn't make you understand. But you will know some day, and there is no hurry whatsoever. Every thought you have had since I died, I know already. *Your* share of the circuit is unbroken at least....You and I are the only mortals that I know of who ever found a way to each other's inner being by the touch of the hands....Our bodies were miles apart—not that *that* would have made any difference, for we could never have done it awake. Never, not even if we hugged each other to extinction! Gogo, I cannot find any words to tell you *how*, for there are none in any language that I ever knew to tell it. Where I am it is all ear and eye and the rest in one, and there, oh, how much more besides!...It is very simple, although it may not seem so to you now. And the sounds! Ah, what sounds! The thick atmosphere of earth is no conductor for such as they, and earthly ear-drums no receiver. Sound is everything. Sound and light are one....Where I am, Gogo, I can hear the sun shining on the earth and making the flowers blow, and the birds sing, and the bells peal for birth and marriage and death—happy, happy death, if only you knew....Besides, it is no longer they. There is no they! That is only a detail. You must try and realize that it is just as though all space between us and the sun and stars were full of little specks of spinal marrow, much too small to be seen with any microscope....Yet a single drop of water would hold them all, and not be the less transparent. They all remember having been alive on earth or elsewhere, in some form or other....The longer and more strenuously and completely one lives one's life on earth the better for all. It is the foundation of everything....Nothing is lost—nothing!"

Mary continues her explanations of how we ought to comprehend the love and merging of soul mates (see also the next chapter), although she is talking about an exception to the rule here. She also explains how we ought to understand merging with nirvana: "Gogo, I am the only little water-drop...that has not yet been able to dissolve and melt away in that universal sea....It is as though a long, invisible chain bound me still to the earth, and I were hung at the other end of it in a little transparent locket, a kind of cage, that lets me see and hear things all round, but keeps me from melting away. Soon I found that this locket was made of that half of you that is still in me, so that I couldn't dissolve, because half of me wasn't dead at all. The chain linked me to that half of myself I had left in you, so that half of me actually wasn't there to be dissolved....Oh, my heart's true love, how I hugged my chain, with you at the other end of it! With such pain and effort as you cannot conceive, I have crept along it back to you...to tell you that we are inseparable forever, you and I, one double speck of spinal marrow,...one little grain of salt, one drop. There is to be no parting for *us*—I can see that. Such extraordinary luck seems reserved for you and me alone up to now....But not until you join me shall you and I be complete, and free to melt away in that universal ocean, and take our part, as One, in all that is to be."

AFTER DEATH (CLARA MILITSCH)

In his novella *After Death* (1882), Russian author Ivan Turgenev (born October 28, 1818 in Orel; died August 22, 1883 in Bougival, France) tells a similar—and similarly mystical—tale about a type of love that is characteristic of soul mates. Since copies of this tale are available in book shops, I'll keep my summary of its plot rather brief.

A shy man named Jakov Aratov falls in love with a singer named Clara Militsch, who likewise falls in love with him. But, because he is unwilling to admit to himself that he really does love her, Aratov rejects her.

Months later, he discovers the announcement of Clara's death in an old newspaper and learns that she poisoned herself. The newspaper article speculates that the motive for her suicide might have been unrequited love. Only now does Aratov realize that he really did love her, and he is tormented by regret over his foolish rejection of her.

From this moment on, Aratov is drawn progressively more and more under her spell. He even dreams about his deceased lover the next night. He decides to visit Kasan, where the mother and sister of the dead girl live. Clara's sister tells him the gist of a conversation that she and Clara used to have from time to time. "I'll never find the man I want," Clara was wont to lament. "And what if you did find him?" her sister would ask. "When I find him, I'll take him!" "And if he won't give himself to you?" "Then I'll take my life. I wouldn't be any use without him."

Aratov returns home and, as soon as he is alone, he suddenly feels a force take possession of his limbs, as if he were *in the power* of another being. Clara's words, which he had heard repeated by her sister, return to his mind now: "When I find him, I'll take him!" Aratov strays into dark trains of thought. The phenomenon of magnetism, he muses, proves that one living human soul can exert its influence upon another living soul. Since the soul remains alive after death, would not this magnetic effect also continue after death?

In one of the following nights, a pale shimmer appears as if from nowhere, and all the objects in the room seem illuminated by a dismal, motionless light. Aratov feels only one thing: Clara is near, somewhere in his room. He clearly senses her presence and, after he desperately begs her to reveal herself, Clara finally materializes in his chamber.

All through the next day Aratov waits impatiently for night to fall. "What will happen now?" he asks himself. "We cannot possibly live together! I must be together with her! Have I no other choice but to die? I'm not afraid of death now. Mere death cannot annihilate me! Just the opposite, in fact: only *so* and only *there* will I ever be happy, happier than I ever was during my life, and happier than she ever was during hers."

In the last days before his death, Aratov repeatedly speaks about a consummated marriage. When he finally passes out of his earthly body, the dead man's face is radiant with a blissful smile.

THE REISINGER CASE

In his book *Wiedergeburt* (*Rebirth*), Rudolf Passian describes a fateful experience that happened to a man named Leopold Reisinger in connection with a scar from a wound suffered in Vienna in 1915. Unlike the two previous tales, both of which described love relationships that continued beyond the death of the physical bodies, Passian recounts the story of a love from a previous incarnation that is rediscovered and consciously recognized in this life. Here, again, it seems almost certain that the pair of lovers about which Passian reports must be soul mates.

In a series of dreams, the face of a blonde girl appears and reappears to Leopold Reisinger. Strangely, however, it is not so much her grace and charm that attract him as it is the fact that seeing her face in his dream evokes an inexpressible feeling of homesickness, a powerful yearning for a long-forgotten past.

A few days later, he encounters her in waking life. Although they have never met before "in the flesh," they both immediately recognize one another. He explains to her that she must be the girl he has seen in his dreams, and she responds by saying that she, too, has dreamt of him. Both are so deeply touched that their eyes fill with tears.

THE FRIEND IN "SAMADHI"

In their book *Der gemeinsame Weg* (*The Shared Path*), Joyce and Barry Vissell describe a case that parallels the one we just presented. The Vissells tell about a man who saw his future wife in a *vision*, although he had not yet met her in the flesh in this current incarnation. In both this case and the preceding one, the couples meet in seemingly accidental situations and, as would be expected, subsequently become lovers. Both the Vissells' account of a *meditative vision* and Passian's report of a visionary *dream* presage events for which the time was not yet ripe, and involve the realization by the partners that they are destined for one another. This *shared destiny* can involve soul mates who belong together eternally, as is the case in the Reisinger account, but it can also apply to a love relationship that is predetermined "only" for this current incarnation. To which category the cases described here belong remains an unanswered question.

During his meditations and visions, the man in the Vissells' study repeatedly sees the face of a young woman. Although the face is the same each time he sees it, he cannot recall ever having actually met this woman. One evening he goes to hear a lecture. Two seats are still vacant in the front row, so he sits down in one of them. He closes his eyes, intending to meditate for a few minutes before the lecture begins. When he opens his eyes again, she is sitting beside him: the woman whom he had so often seen in his visions has suddenly appeared in the flesh!

FIDELITY BEYOND DEATH

In the first two stories, we learned about love relationships that continued after the death of one partner. In both of the aforementioned cases, it was the woman who predeceased her beloved. The third true story involves the resumption of a love relationship from a previous incarnation. The following tale from India, published in *Die sieben Gärten der Liebe* (*The Seven Gardens of Love*), tells of a woman whose love from a previous incarnation continues into her next incarnation. Her husband, who survives her death, is able to encounter his former wife again in her next body, thus meeting one and the same soul in two different women during the course of a single lifetime.

Whenever Saraswati's husband Bhanudatta goes out of the house, she is consumed with worry about his welfare. Whenever Bhanudatta's return is delayed, Saraswati suffers such severe anxiety that she feels as if she is about to die of worry. Her love for her husband is so intense and so powerful that news of their love soon spreads throughout the city and reaches the ears of the king.

The king devises a plan to test Saraswati's fidelity. He summons Bhanudatta and refuses to let him leave at the agreed upon hour, pretending that his advice as a minister is needed on some urgent affairs of state. He delays Bhanudatta hour after hour, and finally commands him to remove his clothes. Then he orders the minister's clothes to be smeared with goat's blood. He calls a servant, gives her the bloody clothes, and sends her to Saraswati with the gory garments and the terrible message that the king has ordered the execution of the minister. When Saraswati hears this awful news, she is stricken with grief and dies of shock.

The king plans to arrange for the minister to marry a maiden from a wealthy family, but Bhanudatta's love is still fixed upon the deceased Saraswati. He rejects the king's offer, saying, "For the remainder of this lifetime, all other women will be like mothers and sisters to me." He abandons his home and possessions, wanders far and wide and finally builds a small hut on the banks of the Ganges.

After Saraswati's death, her soul is reincarnated into the body of another princess. Her father, a certain King Kankaketu, rules the distant country where Bhanudatta has built his humble little hut. Nine months pass, and King Kankaketu's wife gives birth to a daughter named Srimati.

A few years later, Srimati and her girlfriends are sailing along the Ganges in a little boat. She sees Bhanudatta on the river bank and immediately faints. The memory of her previous incarnation is suddenly reawakened.

When she regains consciousness, Srimati hurries home and begs her parents to allow her to marry Bhanudattu. Her parents become angry when she tells them that the man of her choice is neither a prince nor a king, but merely an ascetic who lives beside the river. Despite her parents' displeasure, Srimati will not be dissuaded. She tells them, "The man who will be my husband is sitting beside the Ganges practicing the yoga of self-denial. Only he and he alone is the one who will be my husband! He is my spouse from a former life. Invite him to our home, and then I'll tell you everything."

   The king invites the ascetic to their home and, after exerting much persuasion, the sadhu finally agrees to accept the king's invitation. Afterward, Srimati takes her father aside and tells him everything she experienced in her former life. The king asks the ascetic about all these events, and Bhanudatta's account of the occurrences is identical with Srimati's version. The king has no choice but to believe the whole story and agree to the marriage between Srimati and the ascetic.

LOVE BETWEEN SIBLINGS

The same book that contains the previous story also includes an Indian tale entitled *"Ausweglose Liebe"* ("Hopeless Love"). As we saw earlier, soul mates do not always incarnate as husbands and wives, but sometimes encounter one another in other guises. The following tale describes the love between a pair of soul mates who incarnate as brother and sister.

   A king has seven sons and one daughter named Kalawati. An especially intense relationship exists between the youngest son and the princess Kalawati. They love one another so deeply that they cannot bear to be apart for more than a short time.

   One day, the youngest prince returns home with a special fruit. He refuses to share his prize with anyone, not even with his beloved sister Kalawati. To show her just how serious he is about keeping the fruit for himself, the prince says, "If anyone eats this fruit, or even tries to taste one bite of it, I shall marry that person, I swear!"

Hoping that her brother would forget his oath, Kalawati eats the fruit—and finds herself confronted with the bitter fact that she must now marry her own brother, just as he had sworn.

The poor princess is in dire straits. How can she possibly marry her own brother? In desperation, she steals away, intending to drown herself in the river.

One by one, the entire family runs to the river, hoping to dissuade the princess from her suicidal plan. Finally the youngest prince also appears at the river bank. He calls lovingly to her, "Kalawati, my beloved sister, why won't you come out of the water?"

Unable to look him in the eye, she answers, "No, my brother. How could you ever become my husband and I become your wife? No, let me die. Please don't grieve over my death. Only remember your beloved sister after I am gone."

The prince calls to her, "Kalawati! I renounce my oath. I deny it! I never swore such an oath! Suicide is a great sin. Come back to me. I cannot imagine a life without you!"

Kalawati sobs, "As heaven is my witness, no, dear brother, no, it cannot be!" She lifts her right hand above the water and a moment later disappears beneath the surface.

The river begins to rise. A pale light appears in the sky, and the heavens lose all their color. The youngest prince calls out in desperation, "Wait, wait Kalawati, I'll follow you!"

The water surges heavily. Then, a moment later, it becomes calm again. The river flows onward as it always has. Only the river can answer the question: Where have these torn twin blossoms found their final haven?

THE PARABLE OF THE PEANUTS

Just as the primal human being that originally united man and woman in a single being was formed from two halves, so, too, each peanut is formed from two halves. Suppose we have a bag of peanuts, and that each of these nuts is whole and undivided. Let us further suppose that we now separate all the nuts in the bag into their two halves, return the halves to the bag, and shake vigorously. If we tried to find the matching half for each of the halved nuts, we would soon discover how difficult this task is, since most of the halves will not match or fit together. As with peanuts, so with people: when a man sets out to look for a wife, he soon discovers that he harmonizes with only a very few women. He might be able to find several women who seem like suitable matches, but ultimately partnership is like peanuts. That is, it is possible to put two halves together so they fit more or less happily together, but originally there was only one genuine other half—namely, the half created by the primordial splitting of the primal hermaphrodite.

The question of whether one has found one's primal Thou is difficult, perhaps even impossible, to answer. In many predestined partnerships, karmic reasons preclude the reunion—at least as a loving couple—of souls mates in their current incarnations. The main thing is to allow a fated, faithful and happy bond to evolve. Unfortunately, many people make the mistake of entering into long-term relationships even though little or no harmony exists between themselves and their prospective mates. A relationship of this sort is comparable to trying to put two peanut halves together even though the halves are obviously of two different sizes or of mismatched shapes. It simply will not work.

Mismatched souls who become lovers are usually unhappy together and seldom stay together for very long.

THE PARABLE OF THE COINS

Suppose we have a large collection of various coins and we take a saw and begin to cut the coins in half laterally, separating one side of each coin from its corresponding other side (i.e., dividing "heads" from "tails"). The less common a coin is, the smaller the chance of finding its matching half. This is what Ramala means by the words: "The lower a person's state of consciousness, the greater the number of souls from whom that person can choose a spouse; the further one has ascended along the ladder of evolution, the fewer are the potential mates from which to choose."[1]

This is because the states of consciousness of humanity are like a pyramid. A pyramid is widest at its base and becomes narrower as we ascend its sloping sides. Among humanity, too, the ignorant masses represent the broad base. Only a few human beings have attained realization, and these highly evolved ones represent the apex of the pyramid. Between those two extremes, we find the remainder of humanity, arranged in an ascending hierarchy according to their states of consciousness. The higher we ascend the pyramid, the fewer are the blocks of stone. The same is true of human beings: the higher we climb, the more evolved the souls become, but the fewer they are in number.

To continue with our coin parable, assume that God created only one thousand pairs of souls, and imagine these pairs as whole coins. Since all coins are made of metal, we can extend the parable to show that all coins were originally created from the same metallic substance, just as all souls were originally created from the same divine substance. Now imagine that many different coins are minted of the same metal in various denominations and in various quantities: 150 pennies, 140 nickels, 120 dimes, 110 quarters, 100 half-dollars, 90 dollar coins, 80 ten-dollar coins and 70 twenty-dollar coins. In addition, imagine there are four denominations of foreign coins: 60 one-peso coins, 55 one-ruble coins, 24 one-franc coins and only one British one-pound coin.

We know that only the obverse and reverse sides of the same denomination can be matched. For each penny's "head," we can find 150 matching penny "tails." Each twenty-dollar "head" could be matched with any of 70 twenty-dollar "tails." But we must search far and wide until we find the sole "tail" to match the "head" of the single British one-pound coin. The same situation applies to people as well. Some people have a wide range of potential mates to choose among; others must select their mates from a smaller group of candidates; and some, like the "head" side of the one-pound coin in our parable, must search until they find their one and only suitable counterpart. At this point we should recall what I said earlier about the pyramid and the various levels of consciousness. Nor should we forget that, even if we have many matching halves from which to choose, only one reverse side was originally split from each obverse side.

Sometimes two people fit well together and feel a mutual attraction, but their bond does not last very long. A quarrel or misunderstanding soon comes between them. The parable of the coins helps to explain the source of this mismatch. Sometimes the "head" of a dime feels irresistibly attracted to the "tail" of a quarter because the dime admires the greater value of the quarter. Or else the "head" of a silver dollar falls in love with the "tail" of a nickel because the dollar needs to feel better or more valuable than its partner. Mismatched and unequal couples such as these are neither predestined for one another nor are they likely to enjoy lasting happiness together.

I could continue to derive countless examples from this parable, but I will resist the temptation since that digression would lead me into discussing the problems that arise in relationships and carry me—and this book—away from its central theme: the nature of soul mates.

7. THE UNION OF SOUL MATES

Bearing in mind Origenes' aphorism (stating that the end resembles the beginning), we can conclude that soul mates who originally formed a single spiritual entity will again join together to form a single entity at some future time. They will someday truly merge and again become the single being they were at the beginning. I will explain this process in this chapter and, in the next chapter, I will describe the *grand union*(nirvana) in which all beings (not only soul mates) merge with one another. I have already discussed one of these two unions in Chapter Five and dealt with the combination of both types in the third hypothesis in that same chapter. The final sections of this book, therefore, will focus on descriptions of nirvana.

It seems important to me to emphasize again that the union of two or more entities need not mean that each entity loses its individuality. In the esoteric sense, the union of two beings represents the reunification of two people who have belonged together since the beginning of time, who were originally a single, complete being, and who will again become one in the future, because their incarnation into single-gendered, gross, material bodies only lasts for a finite time. In Greek mythology, this merging of soul mates is personified by the figure of Hermaphroditos. The (male) son of the god Hermes and the goddess Aphrodite, Hermaphroditos subsequently became androgynous. Hindu mythology likewise features an androgynous figure named Ardhanarishvara, meaning "the man who is half woman."

According to the Greek myth: "Hermaphroditos was very handsome and, when the youth left his homeland and went to

Halicarnassus, the naiad Salmakis fell passionately in love with him. He rejected her. But, later, when he was bathing in a spring, she embraced him tightly. She pulled him down with her to the bottom of the spring and prayed to the gods to unite them forever. Their bodies united and became a hermaphrodite with a woman's breasts and feminine proportions, but with male genitals. Hermaphroditos' parents granted his prayer that, ever after, anyone who bathed in the magical spring would likewise be transformed into an androgynous creature."[1]

In the figure of Ardhanarishvara, the Hindu god Shiva appears as the Lord who is half woman. Whenever he is represented as Ardhanarishvara, Shiva is rendered in an androgynous male-female form.[2] Indian tradition describes Ardhanarishvara's creation as follows: "Shiva, full of joy, pressed his spouse so closely to his breast that they both merged and became a single body: Ardhanarishvara."[3] "Another version of the myth tells that Shiva merged with his consort Parvati to become a single figure so that she, too, would be revered with the same devotion that Shiva receives....Although each side of the Ardhanarishvara sculpture features all the sexual features appropriate to its gender, the two sides nonetheless flow harmoniously into one another."[4]

Ardhanarishvara is not the only androgynous figure resulting from the union of two entities that can be found in Hinduism. An intimate link between Shivaism and Vishnuism is forged when "Shiva succumbs to the charms of Vishnu in his feminine form as Mohini. A combination of these two gods is created as Hari-Hara."[5]

"Analogous to the sculptures that depict Shiva with his shakti Parvati is the depiction of Vishnu with his consort Lakshmi. All of these paired deities embody the unification of male and female principles. Sculptures in which Vishnu and Lakshmi merge to become a single figure are less common."[6]

Material that complements this Indian imagery can be found in Wolfgang Schultz's excerpts from the so-called "Egyptian

Gospel." According to that apocryphal text, "Salome asked Jesus, 'When will the power of death be no more?' And the Lord answered, 'Not until women no longer conceive.' And Salome said, 'So I would do well, then, not to conceive or bear children?' But the Lord answered, 'From every herb mayst thou partake, but from the bitterness [of death] thou shalt not partake.' And when Salome asked Him when the truth of His words would manifest itself, the Lord said, 'When thou treadest the husks of shame underfoot, when two become one, male with female, neither male nor female.'"[7]

Hans Christian Branner (1903-1966), one of the most important poets of postwar Denmark, wrote a novella entitled *The Poet and the Maiden* in which a young woman whispers to her beloved, "I love you. I am yours. If you never doubt my love, then you can demand of me whatever you desire. Ask everything of me, my love, make me happy. Shall I extinguish myself and become you? Shall I crawl inside you entirely, see with your eyes, speak with your mouth?" Branner's heroine is describing the highest form of love, an affection so profound that it culminates in the wish to merge with one's beloved and become a single entity.

Branner's novella reminds me of a passage in Plato's *Symposium* in which Hephaestus' rhetorical question is placed in Aristophanes' mouth: "Is it this you desire, to be with one another in the very same place, as much as is possible, and not to leave one another night and day? For if you desire that, I am willing to unite you and make you grow together into the same thing, so that—though two—you would be one. And as long as you lived, you would both live together just as though you were one. When you died, there again in Hades you would be dead together as one instead of as two. See if you love this and would be content if it were yours." Aristophanes answers his own rhetorical question. Like naive children, he says, each one of us "would quite simply believe he had heard what he had been desiring all along—union with the beloved, to become one from

two." As is eminently clear from the aforementioned passage, Plato was familiar with the notion of a union of two entities into a single being and he, too, viewed this reunion as a desirable goal that would lead to enduring joy.

In *Sphärenwanderer*, we receive the following information about the union of two lovers: "Two beings who love and honor each other most profoundly can, quite literally, merge into one another. Even in the mundane realm on Earth, one person often experiences himself [or herself] through the other, sharing sensations, feelings and intimacy of thought....How much more impressive must be this linkage of souls without the hindrances of fleshy human bodies! It is well known that the union of man and woman in the spiritual realms of light is an actual unification of their bodies and that temporarily—not only allegorically, but truly—two lovers can indeed appear as a single body."[8]

In this context, I would like to note that sexual intercourse and its associated tenderness and caresses are the most profound experiences that earthly lovers can share. All too often, people overlook the fact that sexual intercourse is misused when it is arbitrarily engaged in with various and sundry partners merely to satisfy our egos and lusts. But, even when the sexual act is consummated in the context of pure love, it can only last for a limited time, and its feelings of joy and pleasure persist only for the brief moments of orgasm. What lovers really yearn for—union that would enable them to crawl inside one another and merge into a single being—cannot be achieved through sexuality nor through tenderness and caresses. As long as they are still physically incarnated in their present, single-gendered bodies, both lovers must remain physically separate—captives in two separate bodies.

At this point I would like to propose a hypothesis that has often been suggested but not explicitly stated. In the astral realm, the union of two beings into one is accompanied by sensations of the utmost bliss that far exceed the pleasures of sexual intercourse on Earth. The physical coupling of earthly lovers is a mere shadow of the union of two astral bodies. The astral union lasts longer although, strictly speaking, time does not exist in the astral realm. Just as two entities can merge into one, they can also separate again so that one becomes two. Even while they are one, they remain two. Conversely, even while they are separated from one another, they are nevertheless one. Astral bodies are entirely different from mundane bodies, and this difference enables this seeming paradox to exist on the ethereal plane. The souls have embraced one another so tightly, and each has so fully dissolved within the other, that they no longer know what is within and what is without. They have merged to become a single entity. Afterward, however, they can again issue forth from one another and become two. When they emerge, they represent the world of counterparts since "it is not good that the man should be alone" (see Genesis 2:18). Although, in one sense, loving soul mates are male and female, in another sense they are neither male nor female. Because reproduction does not exist in the astral region, there no need for two opposite genders. We recall that, according to some traditions, the first human pair did not possess any sexual characteristics or differences. Strictly speaking, the soul is genderless, "transcendent to all earthly phenomena," as the Vedas say. Like every other phenomenon, gender is ultimately based upon illusion.

When we pursue the idea that earthly sexuality is the shadow of a union of astral bodies, it becomes clear that sexual intercourse ought to take place only between lovers who yearn for a long-lasting union of their separate individual selves and who would gladly become a single entity forever. When incarnated lovers consummate the sexual act with this motivation, their physical union is truly the earthly manifestation of something that is possible between individuals who choose to enter into a lasting union on the astral plane.

When engaging in sexual behavior, we ought to bear in mind that (even in a so-called "one-night stand") we forge an intimate link with our sexual partner, and that this bonding leaves its mark on both partners. This is what St. Paul means when he writes: "Know ye not that he who is joined to a harlot is one body? For two, saith He, shall be one flesh." (First Corinthians 6:16)

To be "one flesh" with another person is much more then the brief liaison that occurs during the sexual act. It is much more than the casual coupling with a partner whom one "uses" only once. One person merges with another not only sexually, but in a far more profound sense, through the union of their astral bodies. People who indulge in one-night stands are no doubt ignorant of this fact, but it is true nonetheless—sexual union forges an invisible bond between partners. In the beginning (i.e., when we were still pure spirits dwelling within the divine substance— a state of being we can call *nirvana*, *paradise*, or by some similar name), each of us had only one intimate partner. This was our dual soul, with whom our astral body was united. We should therefore strive to actualize this primordial principle in each incarnation. It is for this reason that most religions recommend monogamy (as in the ideal of love between soul mates) and regard marital infidelity as one of the most serious sins.

I want to emphasize that the dual-souls doctrine by no means devalues the earthly partnership between husband and wife that reflects the astral unity between soul mates. Just the opposite is the case: the dual-souls doctrine encourages both spouses in an earthly couple to equate their earthly partner with their primordial dual soul. Bo Yin Ra agrees with this view: "Whatever you do with your male or female counterpart here in the marital union of this earthly life, you have done to yourself and surely have done to your spiritual counterpart, irregardless of whether or not you have found that fated partner here on Earth!"[9]

8. RETVRN TO NIRVANA

We will briefly discuss the *final stage* of the souls' evolution, a state of being that is identical to the *original condition* formerly enjoyed by all entities before their misdeeds caused them to fall away from God. This final stage can only be discussed briefly within the context of this book because a more comprehensive treatment would carry us too far afield from our primary theme—namely, the nature of soul mates. Nevertheless, it seems useful to offer the reader at least some information about these matters, especially to help avoid the mistaken impression that the union of soul mates (discussed in the previous chapter) is the ultimate and highest goal of those souls.

As I already explained in the third hypothesis in Chapter Five, merging with one's dual soul is merely a precursor to the so-called *unio mystica*—the ultimate union of the soul (already united with its soul mate) with God, or—to express it more accurately and to avoid the error of imagining God too abstractly or as a "person"—the union of the soul with the *one* substance of life from which we all originated.

The dual soul cannot be found externally, but must be sought within. Similarly, reunification with the substance of life (of which we are nothing but minuscule parts) should not be sought outwardly, but within one's own Self. People who believe in the evolutive principle understand the dual soul (i.e., the counterpart with which we yearn to unite) to be something that does not even exist outwardly. Rather they view it as existing solely in one's own being as a kind of alter ego or

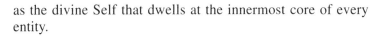

as the divine Self that dwells at the innermost core of every entity.

Jesus clearly states that nirvana will never appear in the outer world or at some particular point in time: "The kingdom of God cometh not with observation. Neither shall they say, 'Lo here! or, lo there!' for, behold, the kingdom of God is within you." (Luke 17:20-21) Nirvana must be sought within oneself, and it can only be discovered through inwardly directed yearning. As Jesus says, "But seek ye first the kingdom of God, and his righteousness; and all these things shall be added unto you." (Matthew 6:33)

The Mundaka Upanishad concurs: "He who has no wish in his heart nor any desire and who knows his Self shall experience redemption in this lifetime. Not through the study of holy scriptures, nor through astuteness, nor through book learning can the Self be reached. Only he who yearns for it can attain it; it will reveal its genuine essence to him."[1]

Enlightened beings are able to experience nirvana during earthly life. Although such people have already rediscovered nirvana within themselves, external union with the divine must wait until the moment of death, when the coarse physical body is left behind. Krishna explains this process in the Bhagavad Gita (8:5): "Everyone who, at the end of his life, when he leaves his body, recalls me and me alone, immediately attains my nature. There can be no doubt about this." During their (final) earthly incarnations, enlightened individuals are still imprisoned inside their physical bodies. Since the physical body is the soul's prison cell, this body delays the enlightened soul from achieving external unification with nirvana until the moment of bodily death. An ancient mystical pun equates *soma* and *sema*—that is, "the body is the grave" (of the soul). Only after the "final death" can an enlightened person finally achieve enduring union with nirvana. The liberated ones melt away, merge into the *one* life from which they originally issued forth. The truth of this assertion is corroborated, among other places, in the Prasna Upanishad: "Engendered from the Self, they dissolve into the Self, their destined place, losing their names and forms, so that one can speak only of the Self. Whosoever realizes this truth attains immortality."[2]

The redeemed individual does not cease to exist, but merges its individuality (which had been separate until this point) with the *one* substance of life (i.e., with all the other redeemed individuals who are already dwelling within this *one* substance).

Walking the inward path is always the first step. Later, in a second step, we can also outwardly achieve the corresponding results. External unification with nirvana is the posthumous entry into a new realm by an already inwardly redeemed being who has rediscovered itself in the Self. Of course, this "new" world is not really new, but is simply the *one* world from which we all originally came forth and into which (sooner or later) we will all return.

The redeemed ones have overcome all dualities. They no longer know any *within* or any *without*, since they unify within and without in themselves. A brief explanation seems necessary here to avoid misunderstanding. The outward unification does not mean unification with mundane affairs, nor does it entail unification with external phenomena, but refers only to union with the divine Self that dwells unmoved and immovable behind and within every phenomenon. This divine Self is to be found within our essential nature and in the innermost core of every other being outside of us. The redeemed ones have rediscovered the substance of life within themselves and, thus, consciously absorbed that life substance into themselves (inner union). At the same time, the redeemed ones have also intermingled themselves with the substance of life (outer union). The duality of within and without has been transcended and no longer exists, although this transcendence does not mean that the outer plane ceases to exist and only the inner plane exists. Instead, transcending duality means that the enlightened ones have harmoniously united both aspects of themselves. For them, there is no longer any difference between within and without. A similar situation occurs when a man and woman embrace each other in conjugal love: they no longer appear as two, but as one paired entity—a blissful state of being that recalls the primal condition that was originally enjoyed by soul mates.

The Brihadaranyaka Upanishad expresses this situation in similar words: "Truly, the authentic nature of the Self is free of desire, free of evil, free of fear. Just as a man in the loving embrace of his wife no longer knows what is within and what is without so, too, a person who has become one with the Self does not distinguish between within and without, because all of his wishes have been fulfilled in this union. His only yearning is for the Self. He is free from lustful desires, he knows no sorrow....All the sorrows of the heart have been transformed into joy."[3]

If only the inner union (and not the simultaneous consummation of both the inner and outer union) were desired, each of us would be entirely alone in the world and all other entities would be mere illusions. The truth, however, is that all beings are unique and irreplaceable. To repeat once more: the goal is not to neglect the affairs of the outer world, but to overcome the dualities of the world through the harmonious flowing together of *within* and *without*.

Because true happiness can only be experienced when we turns our attention within. Arcane teachings have always emphasized the necessity of inner contemplation. According to the Vedas: "No words can express the bliss that the soul enjoys; one must experience it oneself within one's Self." Lasting happiness cannot be found in the external world of appearances because the joys of the outer world are inevitably temporary and ephemeral. Pleasures of the outer world have no inward basis. They fade rapidly because they are dependent upon external appearances. Only those people who have found joy within themselves can remain lastingly satisfied with themselves, even when the outer world seems to turn against them. Perfected men and women bear every blow of fate with equanimity, no matter what the outer world may send against them.

When a man or woman attains realization and finds God within, that person truly becomes *one* with God. But becoming one with God does not mean disappearing into God and passing out of existence. This is confirmed by the Hebrew *Deweikut*, that teaches that humankind does not disappear in God, but that human beings hover before God, and that this hovering is caused by the extreme intimacy and nearness between the soul and God. The man or woman who has found God within continues to exist, but he or she thinks all subsequent thoughts and performs all subsequent actions in service to God. This means that, although the individual still exists, he or she is entirely free from all traces of egotism, pride, lust, hate and blindness. This profoundly religious individual continues to act in the world, but does so solely for the sake of God. All of this person's motives and actions have become *one* with God.

Jesus teaches about the *oneness* of all beings in the following words: "I am the good shepherd, and know my sheep, and am known of mine. As the Father knoweth me, even so know I the Father: and I lay down my life for the sheep. And other sheep I have, which are not of this fold: them also I must bring, and they shall hear my voice; and there shall be *one* fold, and *one* shepherd." (John 11:14-16) Acts 4:32 complements the words "there shall be one fold, and one shepherd" as follows: "And the multitude of them that believed were of one heart and of one soul." St. Paul writes in a similar vein: "Be of the same mind one toward another" (Romans 12:16) and "Be perfectly joined together in the same mind and in the same judgment." (First Corinthians 1:10) Paul does not urge the Romans and Corinthians to extinguish their individuality, but exhorts them instead to realize that there is only one body and that this body is composed of a multitude of limbs (see First Corinthians 12:12ff).

A Buddhist scripture teaches us likewise. According to that Asian tradition, the venerable Anuruddha said to the Buddha: "Our bodies, my lord, are separate, but our minds, I can say, are one."[4]

Thorwald Dethlefsen describes this situation in the following words: "Total freedom grows only from someone who has so fully adapted himself to the order of the cosmos that he has entirely merged with the universal law." [5]

Edgar Cayce says that it is "the destiny of humanity to become one with the Creator, to once again become worthy of Him and to exist in His own image." For a human being, becoming one with the divine Father "presupposes the same state of perfection in which we were originally created, combined with a constant awareness of that primal state. One should not lose one's identity. Each individual will always retain his or her own individuality, volition and reason, but he or she will live those attributes in harmony with God's will...until, ultimately, human laws will become identical with the laws of God."[6]

Individuality cannot be lost upon entry into nirvana simply because no two souls are completely identical. Individuality is needed to create a complete picture, just as each and every piece in a jigsaw puzzle is essential to the successful completion of the whole picture. One piece of a puzzle is of little value on its own, but each piece is indispensable because the picture can never be complete as long as it lacks even a single piece.

The Indian philosopher Radhakrishnan writes: "No two jivas [souls] are identical in their essences. Each possesses its own value, its own role and place in the vast scheme of being."[7]

Origenes, too, does not believe that loss of individuality is the price that must be paid for oneness with God. Without using the word "nirvana," Origenes explains how the union with God ought to be understood: "It is not the divinely created substance of a living creature that passes away, but only the antagonistic direction of his will. This antagonism derives not from God, but from the creature himself. Although he is annihilated, he shall not become nonexistent [in the future], but shall merely cease to be an *enemy* of God and a victim of *death*....God created everything so that it would exist, and whatsoever has been created so that it shall exist cannot become nothingness. It can accept change and difference, it can be evaluated higher or lower according to its behavior, but dissolution of substance cannot occur to something that God created to exist and endure" (*de princ.* II 6:5)

Only someone who has transcended the world can experience nirvana within. This is why perfected individuals pay little heed to the mundane business of the world. Socrates explains that this seeming aloofness arises "because the true philosopher,...whose mind is on higher realities, has no time to look at the affairs of men, or to take part in their quarrels with all the jealousy and bitterness they involve. His eyes are turned to contemplate fixed and immutable realities, a realm where there is no injustice done or suffered, but all is reason and order."[8]

Inner experience can only attain its utmost perfection through outward unification. Although nirvana can only be found within, the inner experience of nirvana is not the final step. The location of nirvana lies, as it were, "beyond the beyond" and not within the sphere of being. The gnostic *Pistis Sophia* verifies this, asserting that there exists a land of light where there are no figures, but only a constant, continuous and indescribable light. This realm is separated from the other spheres by ethereal thresholds that gnostic philosophers describe as "veils" or "curtains."[9]

As we have seen in preceding chapters, inwardly redeemed individuals cannot outwardly merge with nirvana until after their deaths, at which time they abandon their bodies and become completely *incorporeal*. Origenes agrees with this view when he states

that "the divine nature is incorporeal, and an entity who is still embodied cannot be described as similar to, or one with, the divine."
Origenes is only being reasonable and circumspect when he speculates that "the souls, once they have achieved salvation and entered
into the realm of bliss, perhaps cease to exist." (*de princ.* II 8:3) This
possibility reminds me of the doctrines of some of the gnostic
schools, according to which redeemed individuals cast off their
souls and leave them with the Demiurge, the subordinate creative
force that rules the visible, material world.

As far as I know, no religion or philosophical school has yet
provided an adequate description of the state and nature of nirvana. In a tersely worded passage, Inayat Khan explains the reason for this: "The eternal truth cannot be spoken aloud, and that
which can be spoken aloud is not the eternal truth."

Plato agrees with this view when he declares that there is nothing he can write about the highest and final matters, since whatever they may be, they surely cannot be grasped in words: "Far
more it is the case that, when one has dealt with the matter for a
long time and lived with it, it suddenly wells up in the soul and
nourishes itself from its own energies." He adds that, for most
human beings, it is not good to attempt to describe nirvana, and
claims that the effort should only be made by those few individuals who, when given the right hints, are able to discover
themselves: "He who is not related to the matter from birth, will
never attain that relation, neither through learning nor through
memory."

Jesus, whose greatest teachings were always phrased as
parables, shares Plato's view. Asked by his disciples why he chose
to teach in parables, Jesus said: "Because it is given unto you to
know the mysteries of the kingdom of heaven, but to them it is
not given." (Matthew 13:11)

Since nirvana is our primordial homeland, somewhere in
our subconscious we must still harbor memories of nirvana.

However, these recollections only become accessible to us when we spend much time and exert a great uncompromising effort searching for them. To do so, we must turn our gaze inward. Plato explains: "Every human soul has beheld the nature of being, otherwise that soul would never have entered into this form of life. But not everyone finds it easy to raise his gaze from mundane things and recall the phenomena of the upper world."

As we mentioned earlier, the end corresponds to the beginning (or is at least similar to the beginning). Thus, our original homeland must be similar to, or identical with, our future homeland, and must also be our desired goal. Nirvana contains no inconstancy, nor any coming into being or passing out of being. Buddha concurs with this view: "There exists, ye monks, that which is unborn, uncreated, never made, never designed. If this did not exist, ye monks, then there would be no escape for those who are born, created, made and designed. But, ye monks, because there exists that which is unborn, uncreated, never made and never designed, there must therefore be an escape for those who are born, created, made and designed."[10]

134

CLOSING REMARKS

This book has left many things unsaid because it is primarily a discussion of soul mates and can therefore only deal briefly with far-reaching themes such as creation, original sin and nirvana, and because the full scope of these themes can never be adequately expressed on paper. The last verse in the Gospel According to St. John (which is also the conclusion of the four gospels in the Bible) agrees that what can be written is limited: "If they should be written every one, I suppose that even the world itself could not contain the books that should be written." (John 21:25)

Inayat Khan expresses a similar view: "All the world's disagreements that result from differences of religious opinion are the consequences of the inability to grasp the fact that religion is a unity. God, too, is a unity. How could there possibly be two religions?"

The most advanced human being—the one who has genuinely embarked upon a spiritual quest—is never an orthodox religious fanatic, but is able to look beyond the limits of his or her own religion and learn from other religions, and from the world's philosophies and mythologies. Anyone who does this will be rewarded with insights into mysteries that lie hidden in the scriptures of other religious traditions. He or she is also likely to see the scriptures of his or her own religion in a new light. As an example of this, I would like to return briefly to the biblical story about the creation of Eve from Adam's rib. As we saw in Chapter Two, the Hebrew word "*zela*" can mean both "rib" and "side." Merely knowing this fact, however, is not enough: a Christian who is eager to interpret the Bible and who thirsts for spiritual realization must attain more than philological knowledge. An unwary reader could stray into misunderstanding the Genesis passage to mean that the man existed first and the woman was created later. Readers who interpret Genesis in this way would reach the correct conclusion that the woman is part of the man, but would incorrectly assume that the man is *not* part of the woman. If, however, the readers have also familiarized themselves with Hebrew mythology and the Sohar (which should be a required text for anyone who seriously intends to study the Bible) and if they have also read Plato's *Symposium* and the Brihadaranyaka Upanishad, they will no doubt arrive at an entirely different interpretation. The first woman was not extracted from the man; both genders were created through the division of a previously androgynous entity. My commentary on Genesis 2:22 (see Chapter Two) explains this in greater detail.

Some readers may feel a bit disappointed because this book has not supplied them with an answer to the question: How can I find and recognize my own dual soul? Unfortunately, there is no single and universally valid answer to the question of how to find a soul mate, simply because this process differs from person to person. As briefly mentioned in Chapter Eight, it is essential to prepare ourselves inwardly for meeting our counterpart. When a person is adequately developed within and is inwardly ready to meet his or her dual soul, then—sooner or later—that longed-for companion is sure to appear. This is why (as I explained at length in Chapter Five) it is useless to search compulsively throughout the external world for our dual soul. Anyone who embarks on this futile project will eventually come to the sobering conclusion that the intensive search was useless and ultimately disappointing. On the other hand, when a person prepares himself (or herself) inwardly for an encounter with his (or her) dual soul, the meeting is sure to occur quite naturally.

Count Keyserling offers us the following answer to the second part of our question: How can we recognize our dual soul? "Anyone who asks for practical tips about how to recognize his or her dual soul is asking the wrong question. A blind person, (i.e., a person who doesn't trust his or her instincts) simply cannot be helped. But people who have first become aware of their own souls, will immediately and directly recognize the soul of their fated counterpart, just as people endowed with good eyesight instinctively and immediately recognize the landscapes that stretch before their open eyes. The contact between souls is no less direct than the contact between bodies in the physical world. All one can say is: Open your eyes!"[1] Count Keyserling continues: "In one's lover, one really sees nothing but a reflection of the image of one's own soul, so it is no wonder that one frequently recognizes one's fated counterpart at first glance."[2]

We can truly trust our instincts, but we should also realize that our instincts are not infallible. It may not always be possible to be sure whether the apparent "soul mate" whom we have recognized is actually the embodiment of our primordial dual soul. The object of our affection could *merely* be the predestined partner for this current incarnation, or else the person who has captured our gaze (and our heart) may have been a great love from one of our previous lives. In these two latter cases, the beloved could also be identical with our primordial dual soul, but this must not necessarily be the case. Our instincts can err, especially when we meet someone who is very similar to our dual soul. Bo Yin Ra writes about the general problem of recognizing our soul mates: "Here on Earth, only those who, in a spiritual sense, are fully *awake* are able to know for certain whether or not their earthly counterpart is identical with their eternal counterpart."[3]

Bo Yin Ra describes the difficulties experienced by people who are not yet spiritually wide awake. These spiritually somnolent individuals can never be certain whether or not they have indeed found their true soul mates: "Some who believe that they have rediscovered their eternal counterparts will later find that they have erred. And others who feel aloof from one another due to mundanely acquired differences in ways of thinking and feeling are nevertheless two poles of a single, anciently divided, primordial, double entity."[4]

Some readers might be curious to know more about the character traits of their soul companions. Will my dual soul be similar to me or will he (or she) differ markedly from me? Like the earlier question about recognizing our partner, this question is too hypothetical to answer individually. Fundamentally, of course, soul mates are similar and perfectly complementary to one another. In other words, the question can be answered as follows: if I need a partner who is quite similar to me, then my dual soul is likely to embody the virtues of similarity; if, on the other hand, I need a partner whose nature is diametrically opposed to mine, then my soul mate may well embody the virtues of dissimilarity. In every case, whether the soul mates are similar to or different from one another all depends on the evolutionary status of that particular pair of soul mates. Since, within itself, each soul should generate the greatest possible harmony, and since two parts of the same spiritual entity must necessarily be similar, I would suggest that a spiritually advanced soul would most likely be quite similar to its equally advanced counterpart. Conversely, a less evolved soul would be likely to differ markedly from its correspondingly less evolved counterpart. Count Keyserling agrees with this view: "The old adage 'opposites attract' generally applies to people whose personalities are tuned to a single note. Such people tend to be most attracted to people who embody opposite qualities because they find their complement in that opposition. People who are more fully balanced generally find their best complements in people whose characters are similar to their own and who differ from them only in a few specific and mutually enriching traits."[5]

...And my work
shall be completed
when your essence,
healed by the Earth,
unites with mine
in perfect harmony.
Because, there above,
interwoven
in the chords of eternal being,
we are one.
Only with you can I cross
the final threshold
of all times.
This is the wordless revelation
that appeared in light within me.
Come, I'm waiting!

Ephides[*]

---

[*]Excerpted with cordial consent of Anthos Publishers Weinheim, Germany from *Ephides—Ein Dichter des Transzendenten* (*Ephides—A Transcendental Poet*).

140

NOTES ABOUT SOURCES

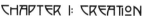

CHAPTER I: CREATION

1. Kriyananda: Essence of Self Realization: The Wisdom of Paramahansa Yogananda (Nevada City: Crystal Clarity Publications, 1990). |4|
2. Die schönsten Upanischaden (Freiburg, 1994), p. 190.
3. Ibid., p. 144f.
4. Der Sohar—das heilige Buch der Kabbala (Munich: Diederichs, 1993), p. 50.
5. Ibid., p. 51.
6. Die schönsten Upanischaden (Freiburg, 1994), p. 95.
7. Ibid., p. 183.
8. Ibid., p. 105.
9. Der Sohar—das heilige Buch der Kabbala (Munich: Diederichs, 1993), p. 123.
10. Die schönsten Upanischaden (Freiburg, 1994), p. 182.
11. Herbert Engel: Der Sphärenwanderer (Interlaken, Switzerland, 1995), p. 221.
12. Cf. H.P. Blavatsky: The Secret doctrine 2 Vol. Set (Wheaton: The Theosophical Publishing House, 1989)
13. Wilhelm Kienzler: Die Schöpfung (Engelberg, Switzerland and Munich, 1977), p. 29f.
14. H.P. Blavatsky: The Secret doctrine 2 Vol. Set (Wheaton: The Theosophical Publishing House, 1989)

CHAPTER 2: DIVISION

1. Hermann Rudolph: Die Ehe und die Geheimlehre
2. W. Howard Church: The Lives of Edgar Cayce (Virginia Beach: A.R.A. Press, 1995).
3. Rudolf Passian: Wiedergeburt (Munich, 1985), p. 198.
4. H.P. Blavatsky: The Secret doctrine 2 Vol. Set (Wheaton: The Theosophical Publishing House, 1989)
5. Robert von Ranke-Graves and Raphael Patai: Hebrew Myths (New York: Greenwich House, 1983).
6. Märchen der Azteken und Inka (Hamburg: Rowohlt, 1992), p. 16.
7. Heinrich Zimmer: Myths and Symbols in Indian Arts and Civilization (Princeton: Princeton University Press, 1992).
8. Robert von Ranke-Graves and Raphael Patai: Hebrew Myths (New York: Greenwich House, 1983).
9. H.P. Blavatsky: The Secret doctrine 2 Vol. Set (Wheaton: The Theosophical Publishing House, 1989)
10. Heinrich Zimmer: Myths and Symbols in Indian Arts and Civilization (Princeton: Princeton University Press, 1992).

11. Ibid, p. 156.
12. John A. Phillips: Eve, The History of an Idea (San Francisco: Harper & Row, 1984.
13. Der Sohar—das heilige Buch der Kabbala (Munich: Diederichs, 1993), pp. 14.
14. Märchen der Azteken und Inka (Hamburg: Rowohlt, 1992), p. 128.
15. H.P. Blavatsky: The Secret doctrine 2 Vol. Set (Wheaton: The Theosophical Publishing House, 1989)
16. Khoury/Girschek: So machte Gott die Welt (Freiburg, 1985), p. 74.
17. Wilhelm Kienzler: Die Schöpfung (Engelberg, Switzerland and Munich, 1977), p. 19.
18. Robert von Ranke-Graves and Raphael Patai: Hebrew Myths (New York: Greenwich House, 1983).
19. Der Sohar—das heilige Buch der Kabbala (Munich: Diederichs, 1993), p. 140.
20. Leo Schaya: Universal Meaning of the Kabbalah (London: Allen & Unwin, 1971).
21. Upanischaden—Die Gehcimlehre der Inder (Munich: Diederichs, 1990), p. 53.
22. Hans W. Wolff: Anthropology of the Old Testament (Fortress Press, 1974).
23. Paul Hübner: Vom ersten Menschen wird erzählt (Düsseldorf and Vienna, 1969), pp. 159.
24. Ramala: Die Weisheit von Ramala (Munich, 1988), p. 329.
25. Joyce and Barry Vissell: The Shared Heart: Relationship Initiations and Celebrations (Aptos: Ramira Publications, 1984).
26. Lexikon der antiken Mythen und Gestalten (Munich: dtv, September 1987).
27. Swedenborg/Gollwitzer: Der Mensch als Mann und Weib (Zürich, 1973), p. 59.
28. Rudolf Passian: Wiedergeburt (Munich, 1985), p. 129.
29. H.P. Blavatsky: The Secret doctrine 2 Vol. Set (Wheaton: The Theosophical Publishing House, 1989)
30. Ibid., p. 193.
31. Ibid., p. 697.
32. Hermann Rudolph: Die Ehe und die Geheimlehre
33. Swedenborg/Gollwitzer: Der Mensch als Mann und Weib (Zürich, 1973), p. 104.
34. W. Howard Church: Die 17 Leben des Edgar Cayce (Geneva, 1988), p. 39.
35. Paul Hübner: Vom ersten Menschen wird erzählt (Düsseldorf and Vienna, 1969), p. 182.

CHAPTER 3: THE FALL FROM GRACE

1. John A. Phillips: Eve, The History of an Idea (San Francisco: Harper & Row, 1984.
2. H.P. Blavatsky: Isis Unveiled (Wheaton: The Theosophical Publishing House, 1994)
3. Ibid., p. 225.

4. Robert von Ranke-Graves and Raphael Patai: Hebrew Myths (New York: Greenwich House, 1983).
5. Ibid., p. 98.
6. Leo Schaya: Universal Meaning of the Kabbalah (London: Allen & Unwin, 1971).
7. Hans Leisegang: Die Gnosis (Stuttgart, 1985), p. 179.
8. Herbert Engel: Der Sphärenwanderer (Interlaken, Switzerland, 1995), p. 197.
9. Ibid., p. 197.
10. Ibid., p. 198.
11. Ibid., p. 196.

ᄃHAPTER 4: THE SOJOURN OF SOUL MATES IN MATTER

1. Edgar Cayces Bericht von Ursprung und Bestimmung des Menschen (Goldmann Publ., 6/92), p. 69.
2. Plato: The Republic (London: Penguin Books, 1987), p. 381.
3. Radhakrishnan: Source Book in Indian Philosophy (Princeton: Princeton University Press., 1957).
4. Rudolf Passian: Wiedergeburt (Munich, 1985), p. 132f.
5. Ronald Zürrer: Reinkarnation (Zürich, June 1992), p. 110.
6. Rudolf Passian: Wiedergeburt (Munich, 1985), p. 198.
7. Thorwald Dethlefsen: Schicksal als Chance (Goldmann, 1/89), p. 243f.
8. Peter Michel: Karma und Gnade (Grafing, 1992), p. 99.
9. H. K. Challoner: Wheel of Rebirth (Wheaton, 1976).
10. Peter Michel: Karma und Gnade (Grafing, 1992), p. 99f.
11. A.C.B.S. Prabhupada: Krsna, the Supreme Personality of Godhead (Bhaktivedanta Book Trust, 1997)

ᄃHAPTER 5: ABOUT MUNDANE AND ᄃELESTIAL MARRIAGES

1. Swedenborg/Gollwitzer: Der Mensch als Mann und Weib (Zürich, 1973), p. 51.
2. Ramala: Die Weisheit von Ramala (Munich, 1988), p. 328.
3. Ibid., p. 330.
4. Bo Yin Ra: Das Buch vom Menschen (Munich, 1920), p. 46.
5. Soami Divyanand: Probleme in der Partnerschaft (Herrischried, 1991), p. 12f.
6. Swedenborg/Gollwitzer: Der Mensch als Mann und Weib (Zürich, 1973), p. 118.
7. Ibid., p. 180.
8. Hans Leisegang: Die Gnosis (Stuttgart, 1985), p. 349.
9. Swedenborg/Gollwitzer: Der Mensch als Mann und Weib (Zürich, 1973), p. 35f.
10. A.C.B.S. Prabhupada: Krsna, the Supreme Personality of Godhead (Bhaktivedanta Book Trust, 1997)
11. Soami Divyanand: Probleme in der Partnerschaft (Herrischried, 1991), p. 4f.
12. Maurice Walshe (transl.): The Long Discourses of the Buddha (Wisdom Publ., 1996).
12. Swedenborg/Gollwitzer: Der Mensch als Mann und Weib (Zürich, 1973), p. 106.

ᄃᕼᗩᑭᎢ╒ᖇ **6**: ᔕᎢᎧᖇᎥ╒ᔕ ᗩᑎᗪ ᑭᗩᖇᗩᗷᒪ╒ᔕ

1.   Ramala: Die Weisheit von Ramala (Munich, 1988), p. 96.

ᄃᕼᗩᑭᎢ╒ᖇ **7**: Ꭲᕼ╒ ᑌᑎᎥᎧᑎ Ꭷᖴ ᔕᎧᑌᒪ ᗰᗩᎢ╒ᔕ

1.   Lexikon der antiken Mythen und Gestalten (Munich: dtv, September 1987).
2.   Anneliese and Peter Keilhauer: Die Bildsprache des Hinduismus (Cologne, 1990), p. 167.
3.   Ibid., p. 196.
4.   Eckhard Schleberger: Die indische Götterwelt (Cologne: Diederichs, 1986), p. 99.
5.   Anneliese and Peter Keilhauer: Die Bildsprache des Hinduismus (Cologne, 1990), p. 35.
6.   Eckhard Schleberger: Die indische Götterwelt (Cologne: Diederichs, 1986), p. 61f.
7.   Wolfgang Schultz: Dokumente der Gnosis (Munich, 1986), p. lxvii.
8.   Herbert Engel: Der Sphärenwanderer (Interlaken, Switzerland, 1995), p. 239.
9.   Bo Yin Ra: Das Buch vom Menschen (Munich, 1920), p. 48f.

ᄃᕼᗩᑭᎢ╒ᖇ **8**. ᖇ╒Ꭲᑌᖇᑎ ᎢᎧ ᑎᎥᖇᐯᗩᑎᗩ

1.   Die schönsten Upanischaden (Freiburg i. Brsg., 1994), p. 65.
2.   Ibid., p. 51.
3.   Ibid., p. 169.
4.   Maurice Walshe (transl.): The Long Discourses of the Buddha (Wisdom Publ., 1996).
5.   Thorwald Dethlefsen: Schicksal als Chance (Goldmann, 1/89), p. 266.
6.   Edgar Cayces Bericht von Ursprung und Bestimmung des Menschen (Goldmann Publ., 6/92), p. 258ff.
7.   Radhakrishnan: Source Book in Indian Philosophy (Princeton: Princeton University Press., 1957).
8.   Plato: The Republic (London: Penguin Books, 1987), p. 236.
9.   Hans Leisegang: Die Gnosis (Stuttgart, 1985), p. 361f.
10. Maurice Walshe (transl.): The Long Discourses of the Buddha (Wisdom Publ., 1996).

ᄃᒪᎧᔕᎥᑎᎶ ᖇ╒ᗰᗩᖇᏦᔕ

1.   Count Hermann Keyserling: The Book of Marriage: A New Interpretation by 24 Leaders of Contemporay Thought (Blue Ribbon Books, 1926).
2.   Ibid.
3.   Bo Yin Ra: Das Buch vom Menschen (Munich, 1920), p. 47.
4.   Ibid., p. 47f.
5.   Count Hermann Keyserling: Das Ehe-Buch (Celle, 1925), p. 241.